Social Issues
in Literature

War in Erich Maria Remarque's *All Quiet on the Western Front*

Other Books in the Social Issues in Literature Series:

Social Issues in Literature

War in Erich Maria Remarque's *All Quiet on the Western Front*

Noah Berlatsky

GREENHAVEN PRESS
A part of Gale, Cengage Learning

GALE
CENGAGE Learning·

Detroit • New York • San Francisco • New Haven, Conn • Waterville, Maine • London

GALE
CENGAGE Learning

Elizabeth Des Chenes, *Director, Publishing Solutions*

© 2013 Greenhaven Press, a part of Gale, Cengage Learning

Gale and Greenhaven Press are registered trademarks used herein under license.

For more information, contact:
Greenhaven Press
27500 Drake Rd.
Farmington Hills, MI 48331-3535
Or you can visit our Internet site at gale.cengage.com

For product information and technology assistance, contact us at

Gale Customer Support, 1-800-877-4253
For permission to use material from this text or product, submit all requests online at
www.cengage.com/permissions

Further permissions questions can be emailed to permissionrequest@cengage.com

Articles in Greenhaven Press anthologies are often edited for length to meet page requirements. In addition, original titles of these works are changed to clearly present the main thesis and to explicitly indicate the author's opinion. Every effort is made to ensure that Greenhaven Press accurately reflects the original intent of the authors. Every effort has been made to trace the owners of copyrighted material.

Cover image © Everett Collection/Alamy.

LIBRARY OF CONGRESS CATALOGING-IN-PUBLICATION DATA

War in Erich Maria Remarque's All quiet on the Western front. / Noah Berlatsky, book editor.
    p. cm. -- (Social issues in literature)
    Includes bibliographical references and index.
    ISBN 978-0-7377-6391-1 (hardcover) -- ISBN 978-0-7377-6392-8 (pbk.)
    1. Remarque, Erich Maria, 1898-1970. Im Westen nichts Neues. 2. War in literature. I. Berlatsky, Noah.
    PT2635.E68I766 2013
    833'.912--dc23
                                  2012035623

Printed in the United States of America
2 3 4 5 6   17 16 15 14 13

Contents

Chapter 1: Background on Erich Maria Remarque

Chapter 2: *All Quiet on the Western Front* and War

Chapter 3: Contemporary Perspectives on War

Introduction

Erich Maria Remarque's *All Quiet on the Western Front*, first published in 1929 in Remarque's native Germany, is usually thought of as the greatest antiwar novel about World War I. Nonetheless, there has been some controversy about its actual effect on the coming of World War II in the 1930s. Did Remarque's novel push back against the coming of war? Did it undermine the Nazis? Or did it actually help the Nazis in their war effort against the rest of Europe?

The Nazis themselves had no doubt about *All Quiet on the Western Front*. They loathed the novel, which they said was "un-German" in its depiction of war as destructive and unnecessary, according to an article on "Nazi Propaganda and Censorship" at the US Holocaust Museum website. On December 5, 1930, Joseph Goebbels, later to become Adolf Hitler's propaganda minister, and many of his followers disrupted a showing of the American film version of *All Quiet* in Berlin, blowing whistles and attacking audience members. The Nazis claimed the film was a "defamation of our boys in uniform" and attacked it as a product of Jews in Hollywood. The film was banned because of the opposition—one of the Nazis' first major public successes, according to Victor Grossman in a December 6, 2010, article at the website People's World. After they gained power, the Nazis revoked Remarque's German citizenship. Remarque had already left the country, but the Nazi's still took revenge. Unable to reach Remarque, they executed his sister in 1943.

The Nazis, then, viewed Remarque as an enemy of their regime and saw his book as dangerous pacifist propaganda that might turn Germans against the war. Other commentators, however, have been less certain that Remarque damaged the German war effort. Hew Strachen in *The First World War*, for example, argues that books such as *All Quiet* undermined the Allies' will to war. Strachen says that Remarque's book fed appeasement—the policy of conceding territory to Hitler in order to avoid war. Strachen asserts that *All Quiet* fed into a liberalism that failed to confront Hitler because "of its own fundamental decency" and because "it lost the determination to enforce its own standards." Thus, for Strachen, Remarque's antiwar stance and appeasement were linked.

Tom O'Brien, in a July 5, 2003, article in the *Washington Times* was even more explicit. O'Brien argues that *All Quiet* presents all soldiers as part of a "common humanity" and that this philosophy failed to take into account the fact that some people, such as Hitler, work actively for evil. O'Brien concludes:

> The peace movement in the 1930s prepared not to fight the last war and, thereby, fostered a worse disaster. "Intellectuals" actually thought history was going to repeat itself exactly; so much for the independent exercise of judgment. Not the composition, but the reception of "All Quiet" raises a terribly irony: Despite the bannings and burnings, did such books hurt Hitler or help him?

O'Brien notes, however, that Remarque himself supported the fight against Nazism. Similarly, Brian Murdoch, in *The Novels of Erich Maria Remarque: Sparks of Life*, points out that Remarque's novel *Arch of Triumph* seems to reject appeasement. The book, published in 1946, is set in the prewar period, and focuses on Ravic, a German surgeon who has been stripped of citizenship by the Nazis. In his study, Murdoch observes that "Ravic and the other refugees . . . know that war will come." Whereas the French and other Allies thought the Nazis could be bargained with, Germans like Ravic and Remarque, Murdoch suggests, understood the enemy better.

Ultimately, the argument about whether *All Quiet* might have aided the Nazis is an argument about whether pacifism, or antiwar sentiment, aided the Nazis. Likely, the most famous effort to link Nazis and pacifists was made by George Orwell. In a famous 1942 essay titled "Pacifism and the War," Orwell argues:

> Pacifism is objectively pro-Fascist. This is elementary common sense. If you hamper the war effort of one side you automatically help that of the other. Nor is there any real way of remaining outside such a war as the present one [World War II]. In practice, 'he that is not with me is against me'.

Orwell actually later repudiated this formulation, admitting that "objectively" tying Nazis to pacifists was wrong. In his reconsideration, he said:

> We are told that it is only people's objective actions that matter, and their subjective feelings are of no importance. Thus pacifists, by obstructing the war effort, are "objectively" aiding the Nazis; and therefore the fact that they may be personally hostile to Fascism is irrelevant.
>
> I have been guilty of saying this myself more than once. . . .
>
> In my opinion a few pacifists are inwardly pro-Nazi, and extremist left-wing parties will inevitably contain Fascist spies. The important thing is to discover which individuals are honest and which are not, and the usual blanket accusation merely makes this more difficult.

In his later essay, then, Orwell suggests that linking pacifism and fascism is deceptive and immoral. In other words, antifascist pacifists should not be tarred as fascists.

Social Issues in Literature: War in Erich Maria Remarque's "All Quiet on the Western Front" examines numerous issues pertaining to Erich Maria Remarque, *All Quiet on the Western Front*, war, and pacifism, including opinions on war and pacifism today.

Chronology

June 22, 1898
Erich Maria Remarque is born in the German city of Osnabrück to a modest family. His father is a bookbinder. His name at birth is Erich Paul Remark; he later alters it.

July 28, 1914
The Great War (later known as World War I) begins. Germany, allied with Austria-Hungary, fights against Britain, France, and Russia.

1916
Remarque is conscripted into the army.

June 12, 1917
Remarque is transferred to the Western Front, to fight against French and British forces.

July 31, 1917
Remarque is wounded by shrapnel in his neck, right arm, and left leg. He is sent to a hospital in Germany, where he spends most of the remainder of the war.

November 11, 1918
World War I ends.

1920
Remarque publishes his first novel, *The Dream Room*.

1925
Remarque marries actress Ilse Jutta Zambona.

1927
Remarque writes *All Quiet on the Western Front*. He is not at first able to find a publisher.

1929

All Quiet on the Western Front is published, to great success and acclaim.

1930

Remarque and his wife, Ilse, divorce.

A popular and influential Hollywood war film is made of *All Quiet on the Western Front.*

1931

Remarque publishes *The Road Back*, a novel about World War I soldiers readjusting to life in Germany. He publishes many more novels in his lifetime but none as successful as *All Quiet.*

March 13, 1931

Adolf Hitler has surprising success in the German presidential election. The Nazis consolidate power over the next two years.

1932

Remarque leaves Germany to live in Switzerland.

1933

The Nazis ban Remarque's books in Germany.

1938

Remarque remarries Ilse Jutta Zambona, in part to help her leave Nazi Germany to join him in Switzerland.

Remarque meets actress Marlene Dietrich in Paris. They have a lengthy affair, which continues after they both immigrate to the United States.

1939

Remarque leaves Europe and moves to the United States.

September 1, 1939

Nazi Germany invades Poland, beginning World War II.

December 16, 1943
The Nazis execute Remarque's sister, Elfriede Scholz. The court tells her, "Your brother has unfortunately escaped us—you, however, will not escape us."

1947
Remarque becomes a naturalized US citizen.

1948
Remarque returns to Switzerland, where he spends the rest of his life.

1957
Remarque and Ilse Zambona officially divorce for the second and last time.

1958
Remarque marries American actress Paulette Goddard.

September 27, 1970
Remarque dies in Switzerland.

Social Issues in Literature

CHAPTER 1

Background on Erich Maria Remarque

The Life of Erich Maria Remarque

Authors & Artists for Young Adults

Authors & Artists for Young Adults is an encyclopedia providing biographical information about important authors.

The following selection traces the life of German author Erich Maria Remarque. The author says that Remarque was born to a poor family and was interested in art, writing, and music from an early age. He was drafted into the German army during World War I and subsequently was wounded by shell fragments. While convalescing, he began to write. His second novel, All Quiet on the Western Front, *dealt directly with his war experiences and was an international sensation. Remarque wrote other novels, but nothing was as influential as* All Quiet. *The antiwar themes of his books, the author says, were unpopular in a nationalistic and increasingly Nazi Germany, and Remarque immigrated first to Switzerland and then to the United States, where he was romantically involved with a number of movie actresses. He died a US citizen in 1970.*

In the first chapter of the classic World War I novel *All Quiet on the Western Front*, four German soldiers at the front are disconsolate after having visited one of their friends, who is dying in a field hospital. They have had to bribe an orderly with cigarettes—the currency of the trenches—to give their comrade morphine. Now, one of the soldiers receives a letter from their former school master, Kantorek, who persuaded the four to join up to fight for their fatherland. The teacher, who is safe at home, refers to them in his letter as the "young

Authors & Artists for Young Adults: A Biographical Guide to Novelists, Poets, Playwrights Screenwriters, Lyricists, Illustrators, Cartoonists, Animators, & Other Creative Artists, "Erich Maria Remarque," vol. 27, Detroit: Gale, 1999. Copyright © 1999 Cengage Learning. Reproduced by permission.

men of iron." Hearing this, Paul Bäumer, the narrator, reflects for all young soldiers: "Young men of iron. Young? None of us is more than twenty. But young? Young men? That was long ago. We are old now."

Out of Place

With this, the German author Erich Maria Remarque stated a theme that would recur throughout his most famous novel, as well as his ten subsequent novels: the dislocations caused by the political and military events of the turbulent twentieth century. Remarque wrote of young men who formed a lost generation that had lost not only its youth, but also its connection to society as a whole. In *All Quiet on the Western Front*, the comradeship of the trench soldier is the one affirmative human quality left. However, in Remarque's later novels, including the sequel, *The Road Back*, and in the final volume of his World War I trilogy, *The Three Comrades*, even this connection is lost in the trauma of the post-war world.

Remarque knew all about such dislocations. As a child, his working-class family moved eleven times by 1916, when he was drafted into the army as an eighteen-year-old. After serving in World War I, he returned to civilian life a changed man, out of place in a changed society. With the publication in 1929 of his second novel, *All Quiet on the Western Front*, Remarque won international fame and fortune, but he was reviled in his native Germany for the book's pacifist sentiments. When the Nazis came to power in 1933, the author fled the country. He lived in Switzerland and the United States for the rest of his life. Although he was a successful author and was a celebrity because of a long-term relationship with actress Marlene Dietrich and a marriage to actress Paulette Goddard, Remarque remained acutely aware of the fragility of security and the impermanence of life; in one way or another, all his writings speak of the transitory nature of happiness and love.

This transitory quality was mirrored in Remarque's own life. As Charles W. Hoffmann has pointed out in *Dictionary of Literary Biography,* "It is sometimes claimed that next to the Bible . . . *All Quiet on the Western Front* has sold more copies than any other book in history" and that Remarque's name "is recognized by more readers around the world than that of any other modern German writer....[and] it is difficult to find a literate person anywhere who has not read [*All Quiet on the Western Front*]." Yet it is generally forgotten that Remarque wrote ten more novels and several works for the stage and screen. Many of his novels were best-sellers and were adapted for movies. *Arch of Triumph,* for example, is considered one of his best works, and other books blend his use of first-person, present-tense narrative and realistic style in the same compelling manner as *All Quiet on the Western Front.* Even so, for most readers, Remarque is a one-novel author, and most critics in his homeland regard him as being too popular to be taken seriously or to be ranked with great German writers such as Thomas Mann or Hermann Hesse. Although Remarque spent much of his later life working to refute this one-book image, he was largely unsuccessful.

A Young Man from Osnabrück

Born in Osnabrück, Lower Saxony, Germany, on June 22, 1898, as Erich Paul Remark, the author later changed both his middle name and the spelling of his last name. Maria he took from his mother, Anna Maria Remark, and the spelling of his last name was as Hoffmann pointed out in *Dictionary of Literary Biography,* from that of his French ancestors. His father, Peter Franz Remark, was a bookbinder. Father and son were never close. Remarque also had two sisters; an older brother died at age six. The author's youth was lived in near poverty and in what Julie Gilbert termed in her dual biography, *Opposite Attraction: The Lives of Erich Maria Remarque and Paulette Goddard,* a "dour and rigid atmosphere at home," yet it was apparently a happy childhood. Remarque loved his mother, who gave him freedom to roam the streets of Osnabrück as well as the surrounding countryside. As a youth, he collected butterflies, kept a homemade aquarium, and became involved in gymnastics. Remarque also demonstrated a distinct inclination to daydream, a tendency little appreciated by teachers or parents. His first passion was music, and he played both the organ and piano. Next in line was writing; by age sixteen he was composing poems, essays, and the beginnings of a novel, which he completed and published after the war. Educated in Catholic schools, Remarque was not admitted to college-preparatory courses such as those attended by upper-middle class youths. Instead, he took courses that would allow him to enter a Catholic teachers' training college. Remarque was not challenged academically at school, and so he read voraciously on his own; the works of Hesse, Mann, [Marcel] Proust, [Johann Wolfgang von] Goethe, [Arthur] Schopenhauer, and [Friedrich] Nietzsche were among his favorites. . . .

Unlike his main character in *All Quiet on the Western Front*, Remarque did not go off in a flurry of patriotic sentiment to the recruiters, but waited until he was called up in November 1916. As his mother was seriously ill [with cancer], he was given frequent leaves to be at her side, and was not posted to France until the summer of 1917. Though Remarque was in the army for three years and was often close to the front, he never actually fought. In July 1917, one of Remarque's comrades, Troske, was injured by shell fragments and Remarque carried the man back to safety. Despite these efforts, Troske died, and this is one of many personal experiences that Remarque later incorporated into *All Quiet on the Western Front*. Not long afterward, Remarque himself was wounded in three places by shrapnel from long-range artillery shells.

Disillusionment and Pacifism

In September 1916, while recuperating he was allowed leave to Osnabrück. It was a sad homecoming, for he attended his mother's funeral. . . . Remarque spent most of the rest of the war recuperating from his wounds in a Duisburg hospital. He was deemed fit to return to active duty on October 31, 1918, but with the signing of the Armistice on November 11, 1918, he never got near the front again.

It was during his enforced convalescence that the persona of Erich Maria Remarque appeared from that of Erich Paul Remark. In the hospital, he wrote regularly and worked on his music. However, his injuries forced him to give up all hopes of a professional career as a pianist. Now he gave lessons and composed. Remarque also painted, and he began to see how he could fuse music, painting, and poetry into a writer's art, applying these lessons to what would become his first novel, *The Dream Room*. Most important, he was developing a vision of himself as the outsider and a pacifist, a difficult role in German society. A soldier's disillusionment with the politicians who had allowed the war to happen is noticeable in his diaries of the period.

Upon his return to Osnabrück, Remarque began exhibiting what friends thought to be odd behavior. Discharged from the army as a private, he nonetheless took to parading the streets of his hometown in the uniform of a lieutenant, bedecked with war medals, including the Iron Cross. Though Remarque claimed the latter was awarded to him for carrying his wounded friend to safety, it is unclear whether or not he actually was awarded the medal. In fact, Remarque felt guilty about not fighting in the war, even though he had been near the front so often. In his second novel he would vicariously experience the events he escaped in reality.

By 1919, Remarque was back in the Catholic Seminary for Teachers, preparing for a teaching career. Meanwhile, he was also putting the finishing touches on his first novel, *The Dream Room*. He sold his piano to help defray the costs of self-publishing it. It is best that the book has been forgotten, for as Hoffmann noted in *Dictionary of Literary Biography*, it was "written in a flowery art nouveau style and was an embarrassment to Remarque after he turned seriously to literature." His teaching career did not fare much better, lasting little more than a year. Working as a substitute teacher in several small towns around Osnabrück, Remarque managed to antagonize administrators with his loner attitude and lack of cooperation. He was also falsely accused—according to Remarque—of involvement in a left-wing, pro-Bolshevik [that is, militant Communist] revolutionary movement called the Sparfacists, and finally decided that a career in education was not for him.

All Quiet on the Western Front

For the next several years Remarque worked variously as a peddler, a gravestone salesman, an organist in an asylum for the mentally ill, and as an advertising copywriter. It was in this latter position that he began to refine his writing skills. By 1925, he was working in Berlin as editor of the magazine *Sport in Bild*. It was during this period that Remarque earned a reputation for loving fast cars and hard living. He married the actress Jutta Zambona in 1925, and started his literary rebirth with publication of the racing car story "Stations on the Horizon" in the magazine he edited. Yet there seemed little in his background to foreshadow the novel he wrote in a few months in 1927, *Im Westen nichts Neues*, or as it is known in English translation, *All Quiet on the Western Front*.

Initially, Remarque could find no publisher for his book, and it came out in serial form in 1928. When Ullstein Publishers brought it out in early 1929 as a book, it was an instant success, selling more than half a million copies in just three months. Foreign-language editions soon appeared—twenty-five in all—and by 1931 worldwide sales totalled 3.5 million copies. Ullstein boosted the phenomenal sales with a promotional campaign that was quite unusual for the staid publishing world in the 1920s, and the book has remained in print and continued to sell for more than seventy years, inspiring three film versions and influencing several generations of young men and women who were faced with the prospect of going to war.

All Quiet on the Western Front is less a novel than a series of episodes in the lives of eight ordinary young men. These eight men can be divided into two groups—four schoolmates who volunteer, and the older, less educated men they meet in the army. Originally numbering twenty young scholar-soldiers at the beginning of the novel, only four of the students survive: Kropp, Muller, Leer and Paul Bäumer, the book's narrator. These four are balanced by the others: the mechanic Tjaden, the turf-cutter Westhus, the farmer Detering, and the oldest of the group at forty, Katczinsky—"Kat," as he is called by the others. As Christine R. Barker and R. W. Last pointed out in their 1979 biography *Erich Maria Remarque*, this juxtaposing of an educated elite with a less-educated but more worldly-wise quartet "points to a strong sense of organization on the part of the author which . . . is fundamental to the entire work and has been studiously ignored by most critics."

In their analysis, Barker and Last divide the book into three parts, plus a short interlude. In the first section, Remarque explores the experiences of a private soldier at the front via flashbacks and memories of life before the war. The novel opens with the company numbering eighty men out of an original one hundred fifty, and closes with that number down to thirty-two. The middle section of the book recounts the men's experiences with women, dreams of what the future might bring after the war, and with Bäumer's disastrous leave at home with a dying mother and a father from whom he is estranged. He feels totally alien in "the civilian world."

In an interlude between the novel's second and third sections, Bäumer begins to see humanity in the face of the enemy while guarding some Russian prisoners of war. When he and his friends discuss the meaning of the war, the older, more mature Kat wonders aloud why a "French locksmith or a French shoemaker" would want to attack them. "No, it's just the governments. I'd never seen a Frenchman before I came here, and most of the Frenchmen won't have seen one of us. Nobody asked them any more than they did us," he says. When one of his comrades asks why there is a war, Kat shrugs and adds, "There must be some people who find the war worthwhile."

Shortly after this exchange, Bäumer kills a French soldier, his first. He cannot leave the shell hole where his victim lies dying of knife wounds, and must listen to the man's death throes for hours. Bäumer subsequently muses about the meaning of this war and of war in general. It was these contemplations that later became the focal point for debate and vituperation, especially among German right-wing militarists and Nazis.

An Ironic Title

The action is more intense in the book's third section. Short vignettes describe the fate of Bäumer's fellow soldiers, each of whom dies. In a short epilogue, Bäumer, too, is killed. Remarque writes, "He fell in October 1918, on a day that was so quiet and still along the entire front line that the army despatches restricted themselves to the single sentence: that there was nothing new to report on the western front."

These final lines of the book in fact supplied the ironic title for the German original: *Im Westen nichts Neues*. Bäumer's death is thus made insignificant; just another casualty, but nothing new or important. English editions whose title resonates with the one-time popular song, "All Quiet along the Potomac," lost the irony of the German-language title.

Remarque's work is impressionistic as well as realistic. Food, bodily functions, and women are the mainstays of morale and discussion. There is little sense of history in the novel, and no mention of which battles the men are fight-

Erich Maria Remarque, in a photograph taken the year All Quiet on the Western Front *was published, 1929.* © Everett Collection Inc./Alamy.

ing—all battles are the same. Officers, such as Corporal Himmelstoss, are martinets or sadists, and when the men beat the cruel Himmelstoss, there is a sense of justice in the action. Comrades, friends in the trenches, die and are mourned for a time. But their goods are quickly shared; a fine pair of English boots are passed down from the dying man at the beginning of the book to Muller, and then at his death to Bäumer, who dies in turn.

The men are cast into a timeless round of battle and waiting for battle, of trying to survive in the trenches and in no-man's land. As Barker and Last explained, "one might all too readily gain the impression that the novel is a succession of nightmarish situations and unrelieved gloom, but this is not so. Remarque skilfully paces the development of the action, interposing scenes of real happiness and contentment, some of which contain episodes that are extremely funny." The soldiers' unrelenting search for food as well as their comradely discussions behind the lines serve as a foil to the scenes of barbarous warfare, making the latter all the more powerful. Remarque also employs symbolism: earth is a regenerative force; a butterfly becomes an ironic insertion of bucolic nature in the midst of carnage as well as a metaphor for the fleeting quality of life. And throughout the novel, Remarque writes in a matter-of-fact prose style which minutely describes the lives and experiences of men at the front in mankind's first mechanized war.

Remarque and the Critics

The critical reception for *All Quiet on the Western Front* followed a pattern that would become the norm for Remarque's later books: praise from the foreign press and mixed reviews in his native Germany. Writing in the *New York Herald Tribune*, Frank Ernest Hill noted that the novel "will give any sensitive reader a terrific impact," while Joseph Wood Krutch observed in the *Nation* that "Remarque tells his plain tale with a sort of naivete which is the result, not of too little experience, but of too much." Henry Seidel Canby, in the *Saturday Review*, called *All Quiet on the Western Front* "the greatest book about the war that I have seen," and in England, Herbert Read of the *Manchester Guardian Weekly* termed it "the greatest of all war books."

In Germany, however, Remarque landed in the middle of a political battle despite huge sales. His book was anathema to the right for its supposed pacifist sentiments and it was equally criticized by the left for being too soft on the industrialists who had brought about the war. This furor actually helped sales of the novel, but when the Nazis came to power in 1939, Remarque was on their hate list of writers and *In Westen nichts Neues* was one of the books publicly burned by the new regime. German critics also tried to prove that Remarque was fudging on his own war experience, grossly misrepresenting the realities of World War I. To this day in Germany, Remarque's writing is not considered worthy of serious study.

In 1930, the same year Remarque and his wife divorced, he brought out a sequel to *All Quiet on the Western Front. The Road Back* recounts the trials and tribulations of soldiers trying to readjust to life in the civilian world. Once again, Remarque had hit the pulse of the times and the book sold well. Writing in the *New Republic*, the novelist William Faulkner commented that it was "missing significance," yet it was "a moving book." The premier of the film version of *All Quiet on the Western Front* that same year brought protests in Germany, and as a result, Remarque began spending more time in Switzerland, where he had purchased a villa near Lago Maggiore. By the end of 1933, he and his former wife—whom he would remarry in 1938—moved permanently to Switzerland.

Three Comrades, the final installment in Remarque's trilogy about World War I and its aftermath, was published in 1937....

Remarque's Exile and Retreat

In 1938, the Nazis revoked Remarque's German citizenship, and he became stateless. Partly through the personal intercession of President Franklin D. Roosevelt, Remarque was allowed to enter the United States the following year. He lived and worked in Hollywood until 1942. In Hollywood, Remarque became a celebrity, maintaining a gossip-column relationship with Marlene Dietrich, another high-profile German expatriate, and associating with the likes of Cole Porter, Charlie Chaplin, Ernest Hemingway, and F. Scott Fitzgerald, who wrote the screenplay for the film version of *Three Comrades*. . . .

Remarque became a naturalized U.S. citizen in 1947, and thereafter he divided his time between his adopted country and Switzerland. . . .

In 1957 Remarque and Jutta Zambona divorced for the second time, and the next year he married film actress Paulette Goddard. Following his marriage, he and Goddard spent most of their time at Remarque's Swiss villa. In 1963, he published his last complete novel, *The Night in Lisbon*, which reviewers praised highly for its compelling story of those who fled Nazi persecution. He was at work on another book, *Shadows in Paradise*, when he died in a hospital in Locarno, Switzerland, on September 25, 1970.

Parallels and Contrasts in the Lives of Remarque and Hitler

Rob Ruggenberg

Rob Ruggenberg is a Dutch journalist and the editor of the web-site The Heritage of the Great War.

In the following essay, Ruggenberg traces the World War I experiences of both Adolf Hitler and Erich Maria Remarque. Both performed acts of bravery—Remarque saved an injured comrade, and Hitler captured British soldiers—and both were injured. Ruggenberg says that while Hitler became consumed with anger at Jews and the Allies, whom he blamed for the German defeat, Remarque blamed the German generals and those at home who had gotten the country into the war. Ruggenberg says that Hitler loathed Remarque for his antiwar stance, which was part of the reason for Remarque's decision to leave Germany. Unable to get at Remarque, Ruggenberg says, Hitler had the author's sister executed.

The British didn't like mass graves, but near the village of Fromelles, on the Somme front [of World War I], they had to make one. In July 1916, in a few days time, thousands of British and Australian soldiers were literally torn apart. From what was left of them no one was able to put together individual corpses.

Meldegänger

The Germans were having a hard time too. In the night of July 14th the allies were able to cut off German communication on the frontline. A British direct hit rendered all German

Rob Ruggenberg, "Extremes in No Man's Land," *The Heritage of the Great War.* http://www.greatwar.nl/frames/default-hitlere.html. All rights reserved. Reproduced by permission.

field-telephones worthless. From that moment on the Germans had to send their messages by *Meldegänger*, orderlies.

These postman-soldiers were running from post to post, "in the eye of an almost certain death and pelted by shell-fire on every meter of the road", as a 27 year old German orderly, by the name of Adolf, later writes in a letter. Every day this young German sprints through the trenches. When a screaming noise announces a shell he ducks into shell-holes and ditches. Another exhausted orderly collapses on his way through the first lines. Adolf grabs him and drags him back to an underground shelter. This gets him a badge—not his first one: he carries already the Iron Cross Second Class for 'personal courage'.

For whatever you may say about Adolf Hitler—he was not afraid and not easily scared. All soldiers who served with him in the trenches of the Somme, and later in Flanders, have testified to that.

Adolf has few friends on the Western Front. That is not only due to his unpleasant character. Almost all his friends die in action—while Adolf again and again miraculously escapes from death.

After the war he told G. Ward Price, an English reporter, how once he was eating his dinner with his comrades in a trench. "Suddenly a voice seemed to be saying to me, 'Get up and go over there.' It was so clear and insistent that I obeyed automatically, as if it had been a military order. I rose at once to my feet and walked twenty yards along the trench, carrying my dinner in its tin can with me. Then I sat down to go on eating, my mind being once more at rest. Hardly had I done so when a flash and deafening report came from the part of the trench I had just left. A stray shell had burst over the group in which I had been sitting, and every member of it was killed." . . .

In October 1916 Adolf runs out of luck. The massacre at the Somme is still going on. The allies keep on attacking. In three months time they have lost 600,000 men: completely in vain, because the German lines hold. In the night of October 7th Hitler sleeps in a new tunnel that runs to the regimental headquarters. A British shell hits and Adolf gets a fragment in a leg. "How bad is it? I don't have to go, have I?" he anxiously asks his lieutenant. But after a glance at the soldiers leg, the lieutenant orders a hospital-orderly to carry Hitler away.

Young Remark

Now the second leading character of this account comes into focus. At the same time Adolf disappears for five months into an hospital at Berlin, a young German enrolls in the army. His name is Erich Paul Remark.

Remark is the son of a poor book-binder and in the years to come he will cross Adolf's path a couple of times. And he will become famous under the name of his great-grandfather—a name he will take on when the Great War is over: *Remarque.*

Erich loves music and wants to become composer. He is conscripted into the army. He does not report voluntar[il]y, as readers of *All Quiet on the Western Front* might think. And neither he, nor his school class, were incited to enlist by a bellicose teacher. He is not 17 years old, as he would later use to say in interviews, but almost 19 years old. But he does not mind his conscription, on the contrary, he is enthusiastic, he feels like a real German patriot. "We are going to save the world", he tells his friends.

In the Caprivi-barracks, near his birthplace Osnabrück, the army teaches him to shoot and how to handle a bayonet. It is spring 1917, the boys want to go to the front, but they will have to wait until June. On the 1st of March 1917 orderly Hitler, recovered from his wound, returns to the Somme-front. Both sides are so exhausted by the battle that a kind of pause has set in. Again Adolf runs with dispatches through the trenches. On March 9th he gets a new decoration for extraordinary bravery. But his rank is still *Gefreiter*, something between a corporal and soldier first class.

According to his lieutenant, Fritz Wiedemann, Adolf is a fine orderly, but he misses 'leadership qualities'. Hitler often looks nonchalant, he keeps his head a bit crooked and his shoes are seldom polished. He does not click his heels when an officer passes by. Promotion is not an option.

A Few Miles Apart

June 1917. Hitlers regiment is moved fifty kilometers to the north, to Belgium, near the besieged city of Ypres. The Germans have gotten word that the allies are preparing a new offensive here.

That's why the regiment of the quite fresh soldier Erich Paul Remark is sent to that region too. Adolf and Erich don't know each other then, but they serve close together. There are only a few miles between Remark's 15th Regiment of the 2nd Guard Reserve Division and Hitler's 16th Regiment of the 10th Bavarian Division. On June 17th Remark faces the frontline for the first time. He is [a] sapper. At nights he has to build barbed wire entanglements in No Man's Land—a dangerous job. Very soon his friend Christian Kranzbühler is hit by a shell. Under a British barrage Remark drags him back to the German lines.

Christian has to spare a leg. In *All Quiet on the Western Front* Remarque gives him the name Franz Kemmerich and lets him die in the hospital (after which Kemmerich's beautiful boots go over to the next soldier in their group). In reality Christian stays alive and will cause Erich lots of trouble later.

Whatever enthusiasm for the war was left completely disappears here at the Ypres-front. Erich watches a shell hitting another friend. "I saw him lying in the mud, with his belly torn open. Such a sight is not comprehendible. And also not comprehendible is that is takes so many years before the full terror really gets to you", he will say later. Indeed—much later—in *All Quiet on the Western Front* (that came out in 1929) and in almost *any* other book Remarque writes about the war, there are scenes with soldiers or animals with bowels bulging out of their belly. As if only then, many years after, the full terror really got to him.

The Battle of Passchendale

This Third Battle of Ypres, better known as the Battle of Passchendale, in which Remark and Hitler both fight, becomes an abhorrence beyond description with gas, tanks—and incessant rain. After hundred days of fighting in the Flemish mud the allies have advanced 8 kilometers, little more than 5 miles. Five hundred thousand young men on both sides are either dead or wounded.

The battle started on the last day of July—the allies attack with all they have. And again Gefreiter Hitler rushes through the German trenches. He carries dispatches with orders to hold out, regardless of losses. Again he appears to be invulnerable. A soldier says to him: '*Mensch, füur dich gibt es keine Kugel*', for you there is no bullet.

On that 31st of July British soldiers advance to the village of Langemark—and are driven back. Scottish soldiers conquer Frezenberg (a part of Zonnebeke)—and are driven back. Other British troops capture the village of Westhoek (near Zonnebeke)—and are driven back. Remark's unit is fighting near the *Totenmuhle*, the Deathmill, close to the village of St. Juliaan (St Julien) and on the road towards Zonnebeke. Remark gets hit by an exploding British shell. One of the splinters penetrates his right forearm—the end of his dreamed career in music.

A second shell fragment hits his left leg, just above the knee. But the most serious is the third fragment: in his neck. Remark is carried away and a few days later he is transported to the St. Vincentius army hospital in Duisburg, Germany. Surgeons succeed in removing the steel fragments from his body. Then he is brought to a convalescent home on the mountain Klosterberg in Osnabrück. Here he will be nursed for fourteen months—until the war is nearly over.

Hitler Less and Less Liked

On the Ypres front Adolf is still doing his utmost best. One of his fellow soldiers later told that Hitler in this period became less and less liked: "He was always deadly serious. He never laughed, he never made jokes". When the other soldiers complain about the war, Adolf rants on about patriotism and the responsibilities of a soldier. "We all cursed him, he was a real pain", a former comrade told.

In August 1917 Adolf's battered regiment is relieved. They have to go by train to the Alsace. . . .

The End of the War

In spring 1918 Germany undertakes its last desperate offensive. Remark is still being nursed in Osnabrück, but Hitler pulls his weight again. On one of his postal rounds in the trenches near Soissons in France he spots something that looks like a French helmet. Hitler sneaks forward and sees four French soldiers. He draws his pistol and starts shouting at them, in German. The four Frenchmen, as worn out by the war as any other soldiers, immediately surrender.

For this achievement Adolf receives on August 4th—for "personal bravery and general merits"—the Iron Cross First Class. This is an unusual decoration for a common Gefreiter. The rest of his life he will wear the medal.

The officer who recommended him for this honor was captain Hugo Guttman, a Jew. The rest of his life Hitler will keep silent about him.

In October 1918, when in Osnabrück the recovered soldier Erich Remark prepares himself to return to the front in Belgium, Adolf Hitler is there too again.

Southeast of the city of Ypres lies the small village of Wervik. On October 14th British shells tear the ground open. Between the screams of the shells the German soldiers hear muffled bangs: exploding musterdgas shells. For the first time the Germans get a taste of their own specific medicine.

Adolf is hiding in one of the trenches in Wervik. Just like his fellow-soldiers he wears a gas mask, that protects against the gas. The bombardment goes on and on—the whole day and the whole night. Suddenly one of the recruits next to him becomes raving mad because of fear and anxiety; he tears his gas mask away—and swallows the deadly toxic cloud. The boy dies gasping and hawking [coughing]. His comrades can only look on.

At first light the barrage stops. After a while Adolf and his fellow-soldiers take their gas masks off and take deep breath from the fresh morning air. *Plock, plock*—a British gun fires one last round of gas shells. The German soldiers panic: some of them can't get to their mask fast enough and die. The others become half or fully blind.

One of them is still able to see. He tells the others to grab each others coat, then he will try to bring them in safety. Among the soldiers whose life is saved in this way, is Adolf Hitler, 29 years, still a Gefreiter. For him *this* war is over. Half blind he is brought to a clinic in Pasewalk, Germany.

On November 10, 1918, an elderly pastor comes into the hospital and announces the news. The Kaiser has fled, the House of Hollenzollern has fallen, the Fatherland is now a republic. The generals have begged for a truce. The war is over.

The blow falls heavily on Hitler: "There followed terrible days and even worse nights. I knew that all was lost . . . , in these nights hatred grew in me, hatred for those responsible for this deed."

It is then and there where he decides to enter politics.

For Erich Remark the war is over too. One week after he was declared fit for service, the war finishes. And then something peculiar happens. When the discharged soldier Remark returns to his parental home, to Osnabrück, he suddenly wears a *lieutenants-uniform*. On his breast he sports the Iron Crosses First and Second Class.

Togged up he walks up and down his hometown. He has his photo taken, together with his dear dog Wolf. He visits his old comrades. One of them, the one-legged Christian Kranzbühler—yes, the same fellow-soldier he once rescued from No Man's Land—reports him to the military police. He accuses Remark of falsely wearing an officers uniform and not-earned decorations.

Remark is arrested, but he escapes legal action because Germany in this after-war period is in turmoil and chaos. In a police-station he signs a statement wherein he admits that he is not allowed to wear an officer's uniform.

He is entitled to the Iron Crosses however, he says in the same statement, "because they were awarded to me by the Soldiers Council. I had to hand in the provisional document in which this is confirmed, to get a definitive charter. This charter I have not received yet."

For these claims not any proof is found, not then, not later—never. Was Remark suffering from a mental disease? Maybe shell shock, today called *Post-Traumatic Stress Disorder?*

Books by Remarque and Hitler

Ten years later, in 1929, Erich Maria Remarque publishes *Im Westen nichts Neues (All Quiet on the Western Front)*, wherein he romanticizes his war experiences. It is an anti-war book of a kind never written before. The circulation is also unheard of—until this moment more than 50 million books are sold, in fifty languages.

Adolf Hitler too publishes a book wherein he tells about his war-experiences: *Mein Kampf* it is called and anyone who reads the two books together fails to see that both are writing about the same war, the same No Man's Land, the same trenches, the same soldiers, the same suffering and death.

Where Remarque blames the Kaiser, the generals, the war-mongers at home, Hitler knows another cause: *the Jews.* There has been said a lot about the content of *Mein Kampf.* But striking as well is what Hitler did *not* write in that book. For instance he does not mention the Christmas Truce, [which] he and his unit were involved in. It happened in those days that the 16th and 17th Bavarian reserve regiments were relieving each other in the frontline near Mesen (Belgium), where you can oversee the valley of the river Douve.

On Christmas morning, right after breakfast, suddenly there were about four hundred soldiers from both sides, broth-erly standing together in No Man's Land: soldiers from Ba-varia in Germany and from Cheshire and Norfolk in England. First they felt a bit uneasy: *Fröhe Weihnachten* and *Happy Christmas* and hands were [shaken] and some dead were bur-ied that were lying around; everybody helped. Then, suddenly, there was a football, coming from the German line. Some two hundred men ran, as young dogs, behind the ball, without a trace of hostility.

The whole day the men hang around between the two frontlines. "I will never forget this view", the Bavarian soldier Jozef Wenzl, fellow-soldier of Hitler, wrote to his parents: "An Englishman played the mouth-organ of a German pal, others were dancing. Somebody was very proud to put a German pin-helmet on his head. The English sang a song and we sang 'Silent Night'. It was moving: arch-enemies singing together around a Christmas tree."

Two Very Different Men

Events like this did not fit in *Mein Kampf* and in Hitler's way of thinking. *Im Westen nichts Neues* too did not fit in—and the writer of that book not at all. In 1933, the moment that Germany [elected] Hitler to power, he opens the hunt for Re-marque. In Hitler's eyes his former fellow-soldier has betrayed the Fatherland.

Remarque flees to America. He has already written two sequels to *All Quiet on the Western Front* (*The Road Back* and *Three Comrades*) and other novels—and now he becomes even more productive.

In the United States Remarque becomes the hero of the pacifist movement—and of Hollywood, after a movie is made of *Im Westen Nichts Neues*. He has love-affaires with [film stars] Marlene Dietrich, Greta Garbo and Paulette Goddard.

Safe and famous in America *nothing* can harm Remarque anymore.

That's why the Nazi's in 1943 snatch his sister Elfriede, who had stayed behind in Germany with her husband and two children. After a short trial she is found guilty of 'undermining morality'.

The verdict states verbatim that she is convicted, "as her brother is beyond our reach at this moment". Elfriede is decapitated with an axe, thus on a specific order by Adolf Hitler.

Remarque Was Shaken by the Success of *All Quiet on the Western Front*

Hilton Tims

Hilton Tims is an author and biographer.

In the following selection, Tims describes the release of Erich Maria Remarque's All Quiet on the Western Front. *Tims says the book was hugely popular and reports that especially in Germany it sparked much controversy and criticism. Some authors seemed to resent Remarque's success, Tims says, while those on the right and the left criticized him for his political positions, or lack thereof. Tims says that Remarque found the attention overwhelming and stressful, though he was comforted also by many good reviews and by an enthusiastic reception outside Germany.*

By publication day, 31 January 1929, Germany was engulfed in *All Quiet* fever. No book until then in the history of literature had created such excitement. The first print run sold out on the first day. The mighty [publishing house] Ullstein, unable to cope with the printing demand, was forced to subcontract six outside printers and ten book-binding firms. In the first few weeks sales were estimated at 20,000 a day. By the end of 1929 nearly 1 million copies had been sold in Germany alone.

Polarized Opinion

The pattern, though less frenzied, was repeated abroad. *All Quiet on the Western Front* became an international publishing phenomenon, selling in its first year 300,000 in both Britain and France, 215,000 in the United States and proportionate numbers in smaller markets such as Spain, Italy and the Scandinavian countries.

In Germany, however, the book, unlike elsewhere, quickly became a literary and political *cause célèbre*, polarizing opinion and drawing aggressive critical fire from 'old school' nationalists and military traditionalists for what they perceived as its defeatist, inglorious depiction of German soldiery. Remarque had portrayed life in the trenches as he had observed it, in harsh realism and cryptic neo-documentary sentences. The style of writing, raw, stark and uncompromising, frequently shocking, was unprecedented in fiction. In many respects it prefigured the idiosyncratic style Ernest Hemingway was developing with his First World War novel *A Farewell to Arms* published nine months later in the United States. Even after seventy years Remarque's descriptions of battle and the physical and psychological wounds of its victims still convey a disturbing, piteous immediacy. It speaks for all common soldiers in all warfare and it was this universality that commended it to readers of all ranks and classes.

It was this aspect, too, which determined its impact among politically motivated critics as subversive. They came not only from the right wing. Leftists, too, found cause to attack the book and its author for failing to take an overtly political stance or challenge the social and economic agenda of the ruling classes.

Critical Attacks

Overwhelmed by the scale of his success, Remarque was totally unprepared for the ensuing controversy, the vehemence of the attrition directed at him personally, not least from fellow authors, impelled no doubt by professional jealousy. Count Harry Kessler noted in his diary the reaction of the left-wing pacifist Arnold Zweig, himself the author eighteen

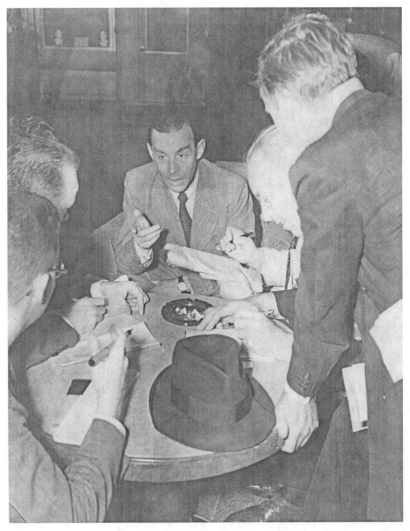

Erich Maria Remarque, at center, faced many questions and much criticism in the wake of the success of All Quiet on the Western Front. © Everett Collection Inc./Alamy.

months earlier of a bestselling novel about the war, *Der Streit um den Sergeanten Grischa (The Case of Sergeant Grischa)*. Zweig 'was venomous about Remarque', Kessler wrote, dismissing the upstart as 'slapdash' and 'a good amateur' who had failed to see the angle from which he should have tackled his subject.

In Remarque's depressive state of mind the onslaughts outweighed the approbations. 'When this success suddenly came upon me last spring, it led to an almost annihilating crisis,' he said later that year, 'I felt that I was finished, vanquished for good. I thought, whatever I write from now on, I would always remain the author of *All Quiet on the Western Front*. And I knew only too well, this book could just as well have been written by anyone else. It was no achievement of mine to have written it.'

More than thirty years later, asked what his reaction had been, he would still remember: 'The feeling of unreality. It never left me . . . I found it to be totally out of proportion. And that it was! Fortunately I always realized this and it prevented me from developing delusions of grandeur. On the contrary, I became insecure.'

The Press clamoured to interview this new literary lion. Veterans organizations and literary groups inundated him with speaking invitations. Remarque went to ground. He had tried to co-operate all he could in Ullstein's pre-publication publicity but the resulting furore cowed him. There was to be no let-up in the months ahead, nor, indeed, were his perceived transgressions to be forgotten in the years to come. The author of the world's most famous anti-war novel was to be hounded by it, sometimes perilously and once shockingly, into middle age. His book became the catharsis of the contradictions in his character: the celebrity and material rewards he revelled in duelling with his lurking sense of inadequacy and instinct for anonymity. He recoiled from the invasion of privacy his sudden fame now triggered.

'I wrote *All Quiet on the Western Front* to escape from something that was depressing me, and when I had finished it I felt free of a dreadful weight of those experiences,' he told an English journalist. 'But now this new terror is hanging over me. I cannot escape from this interest in my own person. People . . . manuscripts . . . the postman . . . everybody I meet, everywhere I go.'

The National Socialists were on the rise and one of the most scurrilous attacks on him was mounted by Hitler's mouthpiece newspaper, the *Völkischer Beobachter*, averring that his real name was Kramer—Remark spelt backwards— and that he was Jewish. It was a myth he tried half-heartedly to correct but which would persist even into some of his obituaries nearly half a century later. Another, with marginally more basis in fact, was that he had never served on the front line and his depiction of conditions and attitudes of the troops there were a falsification.

This touched a nerve. 'The details of my book are real experiences in spite of all the rumours spread to the contrary, which I will not take the trouble to contradict. I was at the front long enough to have experienced personally just nearly all I have described,' he insisted.

He was somewhat placated by the reviews from London when Putnam published A.W. Wheen's superlative English translation in March. Unconcerned with internecine German political polemic, the British Press judged the novel according to Remarque's own ethos, as a commentary on the ordinary soldier in combat, and hailed it as a masterpiece. 'It has marks of genius which transcend nationality. There are moments when the narrative rises to heights which place it in the company of the great,' observed *The Times*. 'So dreadful that it ought to be read by every man and woman who is doubtful about the need for preventing the Next War,' was the prescient advice of the Manchester *Evening News*.

All Quiet on the Western Front and War

All Quiet on the Western Front Helped Define the Memory of World War I

Andrew Kelly

Andrew Kelly is the author of Cinema and the Great War *as well as books on the filming of* All Quiet on the Western Front.

In the following essay, Kelly describes the sensation caused by the publication of All Quiet on the Western Front. *Kelly says that before Erich Maria Remarque's entrance, few books presented the war as a traumatic, dirty, and implicitly wrong experience. The book had huge sales in Germany and was translated and sold in similar numbers in other countries, such as France, Britain, and the United States. Some critics, Kelly says, objected to the crudeness in Remarque's work, and the book was often censored in translation. The overwhelming reaction, however, was positive, and many held up Remarque's book as a true account of the war. But in Germany, Kelly notes, the Nazi's condemned the book's pacifism and included it in book burnings, forcing Remarque to flee his homeland.*

Although works of disillusionment with the war had appeared before [1929], [Erich Maria] Remarque's book [*All Quiet on the Western Front*] was a bombshell. Of the hundreds of books published about the war it was the one read most widely, and the one most influential in laying the foundations for a new view of the war as brutal, pointless waste. The impact of this should not be underestimated: during the war, propaganda was one-way, and even those who had fought at the front had been reluctant to let their loved ones hear the truth (those who tried were often censored). . . .

Andrew Kelly, "2: Erich Maria Remarque and *All Quiet on the Western Front*," *All Quiet on the Western Front: The Story of a Film*, London: IB Tauris Ltd., 1998, pp. 39–49. Reproduced by permission.

The War Books

Remarque's book was one of many published between 1928 and 1932 about the war. All contained a realistic view of trench combat showing the futility and brutality of conflict; all fulfilled the myth of the war: in 1928 *Undertones of War* and Arnold Zweig's *The Case of Sergeant Grischa*; in 1929 R.C. Sherriff's *Journey's End* (the play, though a novelisation was published in 1930), Richard Aldington's *Death of a Hero*, Robert Graves's *Goodbye to All That*, and Ernest Hemingway's *A Farewell to Arms*, in 1930 Frederic Manning's *Her Privates We* and Henry Williamson's *The Patriot's Progress*, in 1931 Wilfred Owen's collected poetry and, in 1933, Vera Brittain's *Testament of Youth*.

Remarque's book was also a masterwork. Like the film that followed, it was highly controversial, particularly in the author's homeland. It was a bestseller from publication day and, unlike many of its contemporaries (though not those noted above), has rarely been out of print since then. The *Nouvelles littéraires* called him in October 1930 'the author today with the largest audience in the world'. After being rejected by leading German publishers, it was published by Ullstein, a Jewish company (which gave an added weapon to the Nazis' campaign against the book, film and author).

A clever marketing campaign made the publication an event, and, following serialisation in the *Vossische Zeitung* for two months at the end of 1928 (the newspaper sold out each issue), it was published triumphantly on the last day of January, 1929. The whole tone of the marketing was summed up in the announcement by the *Vossische Zeitung* of the serialisation: 'Erich Maria Remarque, not a professional author, a young man in his early thirties, has suddenly, just a few months ago, found the need, the urge to put into words that which befell him and his school friends, an entire class of young, life-loving men of whom not a single one survived.'

A Best Seller

The numbers in print, in a very short time, were remarkable: within three months over 600,000 copies had been sold, foreign translations had been made rapidly and it was a key choice of the American Book of the Month Club. Within fifteen months, over two-and-a-half million copies were in print worldwide. An advertisement in the *New York Times* in May 1930 by the publishers, Little, Brown, tied to the film's release, highlights the extent to which *All Quiet on the Western Front* had impressed an international audience with its sales. The following had been sold:

Germany	999,000
France	440,000
England	310,000
America	335,000
Sweden	66,000
Denmark/Norway	70,000
Hungary	28,000
Spain	75,000
Holland	65,000
Finland	22,000
Russia	60,000
Japan	45,000

In all, there were twenty translations in print by this time (it was eventually to appear in Afrikaans, Chinese, Croat, Danish, Esperanto, Finnish, Hebrew (in Warsaw), Icelandic, Macedonian, Russian, Tamil, Urdu and Yiddish, amongst many other translations). A Braille copy was sent free of charge to all blind veterans in Germany who requested a copy. Ullstein was so impressed with sales that they gave Remarque a Lancia car.

Such sales figures were extraordinary: that millions of people were flocking to buy a *war* book at a time when publishing was in recession made it all the more remarkable. The downside was that publishers rushed into print all manner of war literature. In Germany, Emil Marius Requark (*sic*) wrote *Vor Troja nichts Neues*, a 'feeble skit', according to Modris Eksteins, on Remarque's work, though one which sold 20,000 copies. A publisher in Britain jumped on the bandwagon with Helen Zenna Smith's story of women ambulance drivers, '*Not So Quiet* . . . ': *Stepdaughters of War*, which had three quick editions, a French translation, was staged as a play and was reprinted again in the 1980s by a British feminist publisher (there was also a sequel in 1931, *Women of the Aftermath*).

German Controversy, English Translation

Remarque's book was praised widely, at home and internationally, though its publication attracted much criticism. Over two hundred articles and essays appeared about the book in Germany in 1929; the controversy was such that Ullstein issued a pamphlet examining arguments for and against the book, *Der Kampf um Remarque* (*The Battle Around Remarque*). Walter von Molo, the president of the German Academy of Letters, said: 'Let this book into every home that has suffered no loss in the War, and to every home that had to sacrifice any of its kindred, for these are the words of the dead, the testament of all the fallen, addressed to the living of all nations.' [Nazi propaganda head] Joseph Goebbels provided a different view: in his diary he condemned Remarque as a 'draftee' and called his book corrupting and mean-spirited.

The English-language version was translated by Arthur Wesley Wheen (known as A. W. Wheen). . . .

What Wheen did give, and for this he is owed eternal gratitude, is the title. Remarque's original German title, translated as *Nothing New on the Western Front*, is turned into *All Quiet on the Western Front*. Whilst the original is clever, pointing out that death is normal and that one death is not worth a report, Wheen's is memorable, almost poetic, and has entered the language. It may not, however, be original: Brian

Although All Quiet on the Western Front *had been a bestseller when published in Germany in 1929, the novel was included in the mass book burnings that took place under the Nazi regime.* © AP Images.

Murdoch points out that Wheen possibly adapted it from a song from the American Civil War, 'All Quiet along the Potomac' by Ethel Lynn Beers, about the failure to report a soldier's death.

A number of cuts were made to the English translation by Putnam in Britain and Little, Brown in America, which removed some of the scatology, obscenity and licentiousness (particular targets included descriptions of bodily functions and a sex scene in the hospital). The scene where the men talk whilst sitting on latrines survived in Britain (it was deleted in America following representations by the Book of the Month Club), though some critics accused Remarque of being a filthy and dirty novelist. An editorial in the *London Mercury* stated: "'Criticism", wrote Anatole France, "is the adventure of the soul among masterpieces." The adventure of the soul among lavatories is not inviting; but this, roughly, is what criticism of recent translated German novels must be . . . The modern Germans . . . suppose that lavatories are intensely interesting. They are obsessed by this dreary subject, and they are obsessed by brutality.'

The fact that this was not a full version failed to have an impact on sales in Britain and America (few would, in actual fact, have known, and, as Remarque spoke no English, he would not have been in a position to comment). In Britain [English critic] Herbert Read, a war veteran, said it had 'swept like a gospel over Germany' and called it 'the first completely satisfying expression in literature of the greatest event of our time'. He had read it six times by this stage. It clearly had resonance for Read: like Remarque, he knew that the end of the war was just the beginning of the futile search for meaning. He wrote:

> No idealism is left in this generation. We cannot believe in democracy, or Socialism, or the League of Nations. To be told at the front that we were fighting to make the world safe for democracy was to be driven to the dumb verge of insanity. On a mutual respect for each other's sufferings we built up that sense of comradeship which was the war's only good gift. But death destroyed even this, and we were left with only the bare desire to live, although life itself was past our comprehension.

H.G. Wells was also impressed. 'It's wonderful,' he said. Lowes Dickinson, in the *Cambridge Review*, said that readers should not fear German propaganda: 'The book is far above all that. It is the truth, told by a man with the power of a great artist, who is hardly aware what an artist he is.' And the London *Times* said that the book 'possesses characteristics of genius beyond any nationalism'. . . .

France and the United States

In France, Remarque's book was part of an extensive range of war literature: by 1928, 303 books by 252 authors had been published. Indeed, the first anti-war book had appeared in France in 1916: Henri Barbusse's *Le Feu* was an instant success, winning the Prix Goncourt in 1917 and selling 300,000 copies by 1918. Remarque's book was just as successful. One critic said that the huge sales were 'a sort of plebiscite in favor of peace. Every volume bought is equivalent to a vote.' Within ten days of publication, *All Quiet on the Western Front* had sold 72,000 copies, and by the end of 1929 around 450,000.

The book was also received well in the United States. Frank B. Kellogg, a former secretary of state, said that it was 'certainly a remarkable book'. [Commentator] H.L. Mencken called it a 'gorgeous and epical paean to the indomitable spirit of youth. Unquestionably the best story of the World War so far published.' The reviewer in *The Chicago Tribune* said that he 'couldn't put it down. It's the realest, most terrifying, most gripping novel of the war we've ever read, and Frank Ernest Hill in the New York *Herald Tribune* said it was 'obviously founded on indelible fact, and might be an authentic autobiographical account'. By the end of August 1929, sixty-four newspapers—from the *Beacon Journal* in Akron, Ohio to the *Republican-Herald* in Winona, Minnesota—had carried serialisations of the novel.

Even those in the High Command—easy, and often justifiable, targets in anti-war literature—were forced to admit that there was something in what Remarque had said. General James A. Drain, the former National Commander of the American Legion, said: 'The genius of the German soldier author brings the essence of the war closer to the mind and soul than anything else in literature, sculpture or painting.' Sir Ian Hamilton, the commanding general at the disastrous Gallipoli campaign, in a generous review for *Life and Letters*, said: 'There was a time when I would have strenuously combated Remarque's inferences and conclusions':

> Now, sorrowfully, I must admit, there is a great deal of truth in them. Latrines, rats, lice; smells, blood, corpses; scenes of

sheer horror as where comrades surround the deathbed of a young *Kamerad* with one eye on his agonies, the other on his new English boots; the uninspired strategy; the feeling that the leaders are unsympathetic or stupid; the shrivelling up of thought and enthusiasm under ever-growing machinery of an attrition war; all this lasting too long—so long indeed that half a million souls, still existing in our own island, have been, in Remarque's own terrible word, 'lost'. Why else, may I ask, should those who were once the flower of our youth form to-day so disproportionate a number of the down and out?

Hamilton was not so generous as to agree with all that Remarque had written—he went on, for example, to talk about the good that came out of the war—but he had conceded, one felt. He also managed to coax Remarque out of his self-imposed silence, as he felt that Hamilton was the only person up to then who had understood what he was trying to convey (as with his book, Remarque's letters were translated by Wheen):

> my work . . . was not political, neither pacifist nor militarist, in intention, but human simply. It presents the war as seen within the small compass of the front-line soldier, pieced together out of many separate situations, out of minutes and hours, out of struggle, fear, dirt, bravery, dire necessity, death and comradeship . . . from which the word Patriotism is only *seemingly* absent, because the simple soldier never spoke of it. His patriotism lay in the *deed* (not in the *word*); it consisted simply in the fact of his presence at the front. For him that was enough. He cursed and swore at the war; but he fought on, and fought on even when already without hope.

He went on:

> I merely wanted to awaken understanding for a generation that more than all others has found it difficult to make its way back from the four years of death, struggle and terror,

to the peaceful fields of work and progress. Thousands upon thousands have even yet been unable to do it.

Remarque and the Nazis

The success of the book created many problems in addition to the deletions made in Britain and the USA. Remarque was denounced as a Marxist pacifist and his book was banned in military libraries in Czechoslovakia in November 1929, and in 1930 in schools in Thuringia in central Germany by the minister for education (and Nazi), Dr Wilhelm Frick—'It is time to stop the infection of the schools with pacifist propaganda,' he said.

Worse was to come. *All Quiet on the Western Front* joined the ranks of other great humanitarian works in the Nazi book-burnings on 10 May 1933. Goebbels, Hitler's spokesman, read out the names of the condemned authors to the crowd. A Nazi student cried: 'Down with the literary betrayal of the soldiers of the world war! In the name of educating our people in the spirit of valour, I commit the writings of Erich Maria Remarque to the flames.' Just over six months later, copies were seized by the police 'for the protection of the German people', as the 4 February presidential decree stated, and these were destroyed the following month. By this stage Remarque had already been forced into exile. On the night of the burnings, he was in Ascona, drinking with the author Emil Ludwig. Ludwig said later, 'We opened our oldest Rhine wine, turned on the radio, heard the flames crackling, heard the speeches of the Hitler spokesman—and drank to the future.' Ironically, two storm-troopers spent the time guarding Remarque's agent, Otto Klement, and, bored, they read *All Quiet on the Western Front* and *The Road Back*.

All Quiet on the Western Front Shows That War Results in a Loss of Innocence

Tobey C. Herzog

Tobey C. Herzog is professor of English at Wabash College in Indiana. A Vietnam veteran, he is the author of Vietnam War Stories: Innocence Lost.

In the following selection, Herzog says that war stories are often organized around a loss of innocence and a gaining of experience as soldiers learn the horrible truths of war. Herzog explains that All Quiet on the Western Front *is an iconic example of this sort of narrative. He says that Erich Maria Remarque presents the soldiers as initially innocent and the front as a terrible experience that teaches them the truth about war. Herzog also points out that Remarque's Paul Baumer feels alienated from civilians and from all those who have not gone through the experience that he has. Herzog concludes that Remarque does not glamorize war but presents it realistically.*

"Everyone loses that illusion [of immortality] eventually, but in civilian life it is lost in installments over the years. We lost it all at once and, in the span of months, passed from boyhood through manhood to a premature middle age." With this observation from [Philip Caputo's] *A Rumor of War* about the combat soldier's coming of age, we move into the subject . . . [of] the loss of innocence in the Vietnam War. [Thomas] Myers labels this central theme "the personal transformation of the soldier from FNG ('f--king new guy') or 'cherry' to 'short-timer.'" Such a theme in many of the Viet-

Tobey C. Herzog, "2: Innocence," *Vietnam War Stories: Innocence Lost*, London: Routledge, 1992, pp. 60–65. Copyright © 1992 by Tobey C. Herzog. All rights reserved. Reproduced by permission.

nam narratives connects these works to other modern war initiation stories, to classical traditions of the war story (*The Iliad*), as well as to such traditional coming-of-age literature (*Bildungsroman*) as [Charles] Dickens's *David Copperfield* or Thomas Wolfe's *Look Homeward Angel*. All of these works portray an individual's education and maturation as he or she acquires insight about self, knowledge about the world, and a philosophy for living. Underlying this chronological, emotional, and psychological progression is the central character's movement from innocence through experience to consideration and understanding.

Innocence Lost

Since combat is traditionally the domain of the young, the connection between a *Bildungsroman* and a war story is not surprising. As suggested by [Paul] Fussell's tripartite thematic and structural paradigm—"innocence savaged and destroyed"—a recurring theme in much of modern war literature, fiction and nonfiction, is in fact soldiers' education on the battlefield, as they lose their innocence and cope with the fundamental irony that "every war is worse than expected." . . .

As a literary and historical context . . . , Erich Maria Remarque's *All Quiet on the Western Front* demonstrates that the connections between war stories transcend time, place, and language. Published in 1929, this German novel about German soldiers in World War I is one of the most famous pieces of modern war initiation literature, [as English critic Herbert Read dubbed it,] the "Bible of the common soldier." Remarque, who enlisted in the German army in 1916 and was wounded several times, turned his tour of duty into a semiautobiographical novel about the human experiences of war—horror, destruction, struggle, fear, camaraderie, and death. The simplicity and directness of the narrative, as well as the author's avoidance of lengthy moralizing, mask Remarque's passionate anti-war stance. Equally important, the absence of dates and place-names contributes to the universal appeal of the book and transports readers beyond documentary realism into the novelist's realm of theme, character, and interpretation. . . .

Education into the Realities of War

Against the symbolic backdrop of changing seasons, Remarque uses the three-part theme of change to relate three years of Paul Baumer's literal and spiritual education into the realities of war. This education ends abruptly with his death in the trenches one month before the Armistice ending World War I on 11 November 1918. The novel is Paul's war autobiography and an elegy for his generation. Instead of beginning the novel with the customary innocence-training section, Remarque uses brief flashbacks to cover this material and instead focuses on Paul's experiences on the front line or his moments of reflection away from the front, including a trip to his home. As a 19-year-old German, Paul enlists in the army, along with four school classmates, at the urging of their patriotic teacher who promotes duty to one's country as the greatest virtue. Paul, much like Andrews, the American artist-soldier in [John] Dos Passos' *Three Soldiers*, is a sensitive young man who writes plays and poetry, reads classical literature, and collects butterflies. At his enlistment he is eager to be a soldier and is crammed full of "vague ideas which gave to life, and to the war also an ideal and almost romantic character." Such an indoctrination comes from schoolteachers and the older generation of Germans. But after ten weeks of harsh basic training, which forces the young recruits to renounce their personality and trains them for heroism "as though we were circus ponies," Paul changes. Most important, he views life, war, and people from a new perspective.

In this psychological study, how and what Paul sees, feels, and thinks are the traditional elements of *Bildungsroman* war literature. Under the horrible conditions of World War I trench warfare, constant artillery barrages, mass charges, hand-to-hand combat, gas attacks, and obscene casualty-figures, Paul's maturation occurs quickly. On one hand, he still considers himself "little more than a boy," yet his combat experiences have aged him so quickly—a natural phenomenon in the crucible of war. "We are none of us more than twenty years old. But young? Youth? That is long ago. We are old folk." Marking this change are his own heart-of-darkness journey and his strong feelings of alienation from the civilian world. From the innocent youth, he typically progresses to the hardened combat soldier, one compared to an animal reacting by instinct and concerned principally with survival and the daily routines of existence:

> life is simply one continual watch against the menace of death;—it has transformed us into unthinking animals in order to give us the weapon of instinct—it has reinforced us with dullness, so that we do not go to pieces before the horror. . . . It has lent us the indifference of wild creatures. . . .

At times, out of control, he is caught up in the savagery of battle, acting out of animalistic rage and survival instincts:

> But we are swept forward again, powerless, madly savage and raging; we will kill, for they are still our mortal enemies, their rifles and bombs are aimed against us, and if we don't destroy them, they will destroy us.

Alienation Comes from War Experience

During time away from battles (sentry duty, conversations with fellow-soldiers, or a leave to visit his home), Baumer reflects on what he has become and how he is alienated from almost everything and everyone. His only sense of community comes from being with the other soldiers who have shared this physical and psychological journey from innocence to awareness, a brotherhood of the battlefield: "I belong to them

A film poster for the 1930 film adaptation of All Quiet on the Western Front. © Universal/ The Kobal Collection.

and they to me; we all share the same fear and the same life, we are nearer than lovers, in a simpler, a harder way ... " Trapped in the "cage" of war, Paul and the other young soldiers feel helpless and cut off from their innocent past and an unformed future: "The war has ruined us for everything." Seeing death and experiencing the horrors of war ("A hospital alone shows what war is"), they have grown to distrust the older generation's patriotism and so-called wisdom and learned to rely on their own newly gained insights: "we had suddenly learned to see. And we saw that there was nothing of their world left. We were all at once terribly alone; and alone we must see it through." Typical of World War I literature, Paul blames this older generation, including his teachers, for not fulfilling their roles as "guides to the world of maturity" and for not providing young people with a true education about war and its consequences.

Separated from the older generation—[British poet] Wilfred Owen's "masters of war"—Paul also feels estranged from his family and the people in his hometown. Such feelings become especially acute when he returns home from the front on a brief leave. His behavior foreshadows the actions, feelings, and thoughts described in postwar literature dealing with returning Vietnam veterans. Paul senses that these innocent civilians see the war from a different perspective; they cannot understand the truth about war unless they have experienced it firsthand. Thus, feeling as if he is in a strange country, he wishes to be alone, away from the civilians' stares and naïve questions about the war's progress. But he is also upset that these people have "trivial" desires and worries far removed from the war. Innocent to the realities of war, even his mother and father wish to hear war stories. But Paul hesitates to tell them the truth. He fears that the stories will be too upsetting for them, and he also worries that once he narrates these stories the events will be too horrible for him to consider and to control within his mind:

> I realize he [Paul's father] does not know that a man cannot talk of such things; I would do it willingly, but it is too dangerous for me to put these things into words. I am afraid they might become gigantic and I be no longer able to master them. What would become of us if everything that happens out there were quite clear to us?

Realism and Stoicism

After recognizing his loss of innocence and confronting the metaphysical darkness of his war experiences, Paul must develop a way to cope with his thoughts, feelings, and experiences—a philosophy for living with war. Like the typical combat soldier, he tries to control his environment as well as his thoughts, by developing a protective combat numbness. He becomes preoccupied with the surface realities of his existence—food, shelter, mail, rest, and the daily routines of war—at the expense of the horrible truths and painful feelings. His commitments become quite simple—his and his friends' survival. During moments of controlled reflection, however, he ponders his spiritual isolation, weariness, loss of hope, bleak future after the war, and the extent of his change: "I believe we are lost." Yet, armed with this knowledge, he ... chooses not a separate peace, leaving the war, but a realistic perspective and a stoic acceptance of his situation:

> But for all that we were no mutineers, no deserters, no cowards.... We loved our country as much as they [civilians]; we went courageously into every action; but also we distinguished the false from the true, we had suddenly learned to see.

Remarque certainly presents nothing glamorous or comforting about the war described in this novel, and he does not temper the brutal realism of the battlefield with the momentary attractions of combat. Paul's death is described briefly and unceremoniously: "He fell in October 1918, on a day that was so quiet and still ... " Remarque's war story is one that current readers continue to find relevant, moving, and truthful.

All Quiet on the Western Front Is Crude and Misleading

J.C. Squire

J.C. Squire was a British poet, writer, historian, and literary editor. He edited the London Mercury *literary journal from 1919 to 1934.*

In the following selection, Squire argues that All Quiet on the Western Front *and other similar German war books are excessively and unnecessarily crude, especially in their depictions of bodily functions and latrines. He says the German war books also present Germans too sympathetically, when the truth is that Germans are a cruel, perverted, and militaristic people. He maintains that Germans will not write the great novel of the war.*

The world, lately [about 1929], has been flooded with war-books, mostly from Germany. Of the English war-books, undoubtedly the best is [W.F. Morris's] *Bretherton*; Mr. Richard Aldington's *Death of a Hero* ([published by] Chatto) has some very fine and convincing pictures of the war at the end, but the earlier chapters are so puerile in their assault upon exploded conventions, and their denial of immutable facts, that it must take a very courageous and sympathetic reader to get to the end. Mr. Aldington appears to have "found out" woman: it is better to find woman. He has also found out patriotism, wisdom, realism, idealism, reticence and frankness: he is bewildered and screams, sometimes (owing to his publishers' squeamishness) in asterisks. It is an extraordinary thing that young authors should suppose that they are the first who have

J.C. Squire, "Editorial Notes," *The London Mercury*, vol. 21, no. 121, November 1929–1930, pp. 2–4.

ever heard of blasphemous or obscene words, and that no-body before them has candidly considered the functions of the body, and of set intent decided not to dwell upon them in literature.

The Lavatory School

"Criticism," said [French novelist] Anatole France, "is the adventure of the soul among masterpieces." The adventure of the soul among lavatories is not inviting: but this, roughly, is what criticism of recent translated German novels must be. Our own more daring authors seem to imagine that nobody before them has ever heard of a lavatory, and that the Victorians pretended, even to themselves, that they had no digestive systems. The modern Germans are not quite in that state: they merely suppose that lavatories are intensely interesting. They are obsessed by this dreary subject; and they are obsessed by brutality. They would not be obsessed by brutality if they had not seen so much of it. The old German Army was notoriously brutal ... but, according to the books, the German Army in war-time seems to have been just as bad. Every book we read contains the same attacks upon the selfish indulgence of officers and the vile cruelty of non-commissioned-officers, which (if the books be evidence) was extended to the exhausted men in the trenches and even to the wounded. By the same token the authors of these books seem to be strangely fascinated by brutality. Dirt and suffering seem to be their main preoccupation.

The most talked-of of the German war-books has been *All Quiet on the Western Front*. Whoever invented this English title had a touch of genius: he probably remembered the old, ironic "All is quiet in Warsaw," which implied suppression and death. The title would have sold any book: the opening, in which we were introduced to a row of lavatories, clinched the matter. Yet it wasn't a very good book. There were moving chapters (nobody can help being moved by the slow death of

a nameless person, adult or child . . .) and there were "bold"
chapters in which it was admitted that shells tear and torture
the nameless and that there are men and women who, particularly under the shadow of death, will indulge in casual for-
nication. But the author had no sense of humour, little sense
of character, no sense at all (for all his machine-made background of pseudo-philosophy) of the eternal issues involved,
or of the souls of the enemy. *War,* by Ludwig Renn, which
covered much the same ground—following a platoon through
the war—was much better: it had an enterprising title and has
been overshadowed by Herr Remarque's book. *Class 1902* is
not better, but it has its interest for a student of German
mentality. It describes the childhood of a boy in a West German town who was twelve when the war broke out. Most of
his time seems to have been spent in trying to discover facts
about the "mystery" of sexual connection: his obsession re-
garding this theme will appear no more remarkable to the ordinary Englishman than the fact that he never really knew "all
about it" until he was seventeen. This book, though written by
a person whom we should regard as stupid, does give a picture of Germany in the late war-years which is confirmed
from other sources: a Germany of hunger, neurotic cruelty,
and despairing lasciviousness—always tinged, or painted, by
German sentimentality (alas, that so little of it remains!) about
mill-wheels, rippling streams, spring and the nightingales. The
best of the German war- books so far (excluding [Arnold
Zweig's *The Case of Sergeant*] *Grischa*, which is only inciden-
tally about the war) is undoubtedly *Schlump*. This book is
anonymous. Its author, who (in spite of his frank confessions
about his thefts, profiteering and amours) does not come to
life (as do the villains Cellini and Casanova), was a boy of
seventeen when the war broke out, went to France as a private
in command of three occupied villages, then had a spell of
quite ghastly work in the trenches, and finished as a comfort-
able administrator in Belgium, retiring to Germany with the

army that flooded the Belgian roads just as the Kaiser was dashing across the Dutch frontier with a fleet of fast motor-cars. The hook has the usual German lack of a code, and it is written in the fashionable short, jerky, realistic sentences in which a murder is given six words just as a tea-party is. But it has one gloriously Rabelaisian[1] episode, it is lucid, and it does contain the best descriptions we have ever seen of the life of the infantry in the frozen, bombarded trenches.

German and English War-Books

Not one of these books is a masterpiece: not one of these books has been written by a man with a first-class brain, a heart, an artist's gifts and a general compassion. We do doubt (though we are subject to correction by facts) whether the really great book about the war will come from Germany. Nations do not change their characteristics in a few years: this nation has produced nothing in art since [fifteenth-century painter Albrecht] Dürer, and hardly anything in literature: and, as for its music, it has almost all been produced by South Germans and Jews, the Prussian domination[2] spelling death to the human spirit. That the "young" should wish to read the German records and consider the German case is only natural: we fought these people and why should everything be taken on trust from the elders? But the "young" may ultimately get over their Rousseauism [that is, their belief in innocence and romanticism] and even their admirable sympathy with a beaten enemy, and learn to look facts in the face. The facts are that the German nation is more permeated by all the perversions in the text-books than any other race on earth; that they have never yet understood the minds of other

1. François Rabelais was a Renaissance French author known for grotesque, bawdy jokes.

2. Prussia was a German kingdom that conquered all of Germany in the 1800s and was known for its militarism.

peoples, or even tried to; and that, when they escape from sci-
entific materialism into "religion", they worship a "good old
German God" who is indistinguishable from the disgusting
tribal deity whose jealousy, partisanship, and arbitrary cruelty
makes the Old Testament such depressing reading to anybody
who has in any degree imbibed the principles of the New
[Testament]. In none of these German war-books do we feel
any sense of the general interests of the world, or any appreciation of the broad foundations of morality, whether individual or national.

It will not come from a German, though at the moment
we may be curious as to what was going on on the other side
of the curtain. If it is to come from an Englishman we do not
yet know from whom. We have had a few very good books
about the War, which have faced the torments both of the
flesh and of the spirit, but we have not yet had a novel or an
epic which has shown both the general outlines of the struggle
against the eternal and puzzling background and the individual agonies of the man in the trench. Modern war does not
lend itself to the sentimental treatment of the old adventure-
story writer who thought in terms of grown-up boy-scouts,
and only occasionally had to envisage a death from a clean
bullet wound through the forehead. But the whole truth has
not been told when we are given a series of pictures (though
these pictures, for the sake of the future, must always be given)
of wounded men crying for their mothers on the wire, of men
still living with their skulls shot off, of astonished men hold-
ing their entrails in their hands and dying from shock. And
these things must be remembered, and depicted, and depicted
again: however much the men who saw them may shrink
from them it is their duty to speak. But speech out of hysteria
is not better than speech "motivated" by a desire to shock and
exploit: it must come from a religious man and a lover of his
kind. And it may be that the novel of this war (there is prece-
dent for it) may come from some [Leo] Tolstoi [author of

War and Peace] or [Thomas] Hardy [author of *Return of the Native*] of the future who never saw a bullet fired and has never looked on the face of the unnecessarily dead.

In Its German Context, *All Quiet on the Western Front* Is a Pacifist Novel

Brian Murdoch

Brian Murdoch is emeritus professor of German at the University of Stirling, Scotland.

In the following essay, Murdoch argues that All Quiet on the Western Front *was specifically aimed at its German audience in the Weimar Republic of the late 1920s. For example, Murdoch says, Paul Bäumer's innocence, the lack of focus on the enemies, and the difficulty in articulating the causes of the war are all hallmarks of Weimar literature. Murdoch asserts that the book, in its Weimar context, is clearly pacifist and condemns all wars. War in the novel, he says, is shown as terrible and is blamed on military and political leaders.*

Im Westen nichts Neues [the German title of *All Quiet on the Western Front*] provokes thought about the nature of war in various different ways. The most obvious is the direct presentation of the horrors: parts of bodies hanging in trees, the wounded soldier calling out from no man's land, the slow gurgling death of the French soldier. Sometimes the telegrammatic lists of forms of attack, or weapons, or types of wounds make their point. The reader is, however, also prompted to consider the nature of war by being privy to the inconclusive and often humorous discussions by the young or uneducated soldiers. Thus when the visit of the Kaiser [the German leader] leads to a discussion between the *Gymnasium* pupils and the working-class soldiers of how wars come about, one of the

Brian Murdoch, "2: From the Frog's Perspective," *The Novels of Erich Maria Remarque: Sparks of Life*, New York: Camden House, 2006, pp. 44–47. Copyright © 2006 by Brian Murdoch. All rights reserved. Reproduced by permission.

former declares that wars happen when one country insults another. The answer comes that it is impossible for a mountain to insult another mountain; when this is countered by the fact that a nation can be insulted, Tjaden—not one of the high school group—points out that he does not feel insulted and should therefore not be there. The only people to profit from war, the soldiers feel at this point, are those like the Kaiser, who need a famous victory. Of course there is no conclusion. Müller comments that it is better that the war should be fought in France than in Germany, and Tjaden responds that the best of all would be no war at all. Eventually a consensus is reached that the discussion is pointless because it will change nothing. This may be true in the immediate historical context; the message to the Weimar reader, though, is that perhaps things might be changed.

Led Past the Bed

Sometimes [narrator Paul] Bäumer's comments are addressed directly to the reader. In the second chapter the soldiers visit Franz Kemmerich, who is dying in a field hospital, and Bäumer thinks:

> Da liegt er nun, weshalb nur? Man sollte die ganze Welt an diesem Bette vorbeifuhren und sagen: Das ist Franz Kemmerich, neunzehneinhalb Jahre alt, er will nicht sterben. Lasst ihn nicht sterben!

> [Now he is lying there—and for what reason? Everybody in the whole world ought to be made to walk past his bed and be told: "This is Franz Kemmerich; he's nineteen and a half, and he doesn't want to die! Don't let him die!"]

The novel has done precisely what Bäumer has asked: the world has been led past that bed. Later, when he is in a *Lazarett* (military hospital) himself, Bäumer makes a personal statement that gradually develops into a philosophical attitude to the war as a whole:

> Ich bin jung, ich bin zwanzig Jahre alt; aber ich kenne vom
> Leben nichts anderes als die Verzweiflung, den Tod, die Angst
> und die Verkettung sinnlosester Oberflächlichkeit mit einem
> Abgrund des Leidens. Ich sehe, dass Völker gegeneinander
> getrieben werden und sich schweigend, unwissend, töricht,
> gehorsam, unschuldig töten.

> [I am young, I am twenty years of age; but I know nothing
> of life except despair, death, fear, and the combination of
> completely mindless superficiality with an abyss of suffering.
> I see people being driven against one another, and silently,
> uncomprehendingly, foolishly, and obediently and inno-
> cently killing one another.]

Most striking is the idea of the victim as killer, the paradoxical
unschuldig töten (innocently killing). These almost exculpatory
words are again clearly directed at the ex-soldiers who survived the war. Bäumer also wonders how the older generation
would react if they called them to account. This, too, is what
the novel is doing.

War Is War

Often Bäumer himself is unable to think things through because, since he is actually in the war, those conclusions would
lead to madness. For the time being he is forced to cling to
the circular statement that "war is war"; sometimes, however,
Bäumer decides consciously to store up ideas for later, and
thus Remarque permits him to present ideas directly to the
later readership. When on guard-duty over the Russian prisoners, for example, he has time to speculate.

> Ein Befehl hat diese stille Gestalten zu unseren Feinden
> gemacht; ein Befehl könnte sie in unsere Freude verwandeln.
> An irgendeinem Tisch wird ein Schriftstück von einigen
> Leuten unterzeichnet, die keiner von uns kennt; und jahr-
> elang ist unser höchstes Ziel das, worauf sonst die Veracht-
> ung der Welt und ihre höchste Strafe ruht.

Paul Bäumer was played by Lew Ayres in the film version of All Quiet on the Western Front. © John Springer Collection/Corbis.

[An order has turned these silent figures into our enemies; an order could turn them into friends again. On some table, a document is signed by some people that none of us knows, and for years our main aim in life is the one thing that usually draws the condemnation of the whole world and incurs its severest punishment in law.]

Bäumer stops: "Hier darf ich nicht weiterdenken" (I mustn't think along those lines any more), but the importance of this passage for the novel and for Weimar is clear. . . .

The Novel's Anti-War Message

A war implies an enemy. For Bäumer, however, the principal enemy faced by all soldiers is death itself, and after that the bullying noncommissioned officers of their own army. The declared enemy—the British or French soldiers—are usually invisible, although we are aware of their guns. Bäumer himself meets only the *poilu* Duval and the Russian prisoners of war whom he guards. The absence of a specific enemy was a programmatic policy message for the Weimar Republic. The consistent portrayal of Bäumer as a victim, who was too young to be involved even with the hysteria associated with the outbreak in 1914, and who understands little and can influence even less, is also appropriate to the novel's Weimar context and to the generation that survived the war. The Weimar Republic welcomed the realistic and graphic presentation of the horrors of the war in a way that showed the participants free of responsibility, if not of guilt. Other unresponsible and even guilt-free narrators and protagonists in Weimar anti-war novels of the period include stretcher bearers, women, children, or schoolboys too young to join up, and most extreme of all, but most clearly a participant who is an innocent victim of bestial humanity, Liesl the mare, used as the narrator in Ernst Johannsen's unjustly forgotten *Fronterinnerungen cines Pferdes* (Front Line Memoirs of a Horse). What unites all these involved narrators is the complete lack of awareness of the reasons for war as such, or for this war.

Im Westen nichts Neues needs more than any of Remarque's later works to be located in various contexts, first of all in the genre of the war novel. This itself, however, requires some subdivision: *Im Westen nichts Neues* is a novel about the First World War, but not one written either during that war, like

Henri Barbusse's *Le Feu* (*Under Fire*), or just afterwards, such as Ernst Jünger's *In Stahlgewittern* (*Storm of Steel*), nor, on the other hand, at a historical distance so far removed as to be completely divorced from the actual experience (as with recent novels by, for example, Pat Barker). It is a historical novel addressing as its first audience Germans who shared the experiences presented in the work and survived, and it can be contextualized therefore as Weimar literature and hence is a German novel for reasons other than the simply linguistic. As one of the many novels produced at around the same time that took a similarly pacifist and anti-war stance, however, it is both national and international. *Im Westen nichts Neues* is a German novel in that it shows us German soldiers worn down to what amounts to a defeat in 1918. The war in the novel has no beginning, nor do we see the end, because Bäumer dies before the armistice, so that questions of responsibility and indeed of whether or not Germany was ultimately defeated are not raised. It is also worth noting—though the Nazi critics again missed the point—that there is no lack of patriotism in general terms on the part of Remarque's soldiers. All these elements would have elicited a response from those in the Weimar Republic trying to come to terms with the war. At the same time, the intentional internationalism of the novel is clear in the presentation precisely from the viewpoint of the ordinary soldier and member of the lost generation. Equally clear is the expressly pacifist message. In fact, some English-language reviews criticized the novel for offering too mild a presentation of the German soldier. Nevertheless, the work is a clear indictment of all wars. Wars are still fought, even if not in the trenches, and they still give rise to political chaos. They are still fought largely by the young and uncomprehending, who are themselves forced by killing to incur a guilt that they do not necessarily deserve, while the major questions, such as why wars happen at all, often still go unanswered. One criticism of the work was that Remarque did not take a political stand, which means that he did not allow Bäumer to do so. This is partly justified by the consistent character of the narrator, but in fact the work does have a political dimension in various respects. Its pacifist stance and the emphasis on the soldiers as victims of the war are both contributions to the political agenda of Weimar Germany, and in general terms, the attacks on a prewar social system embodied in teachers like Kantorek, and the references to the capitalist profiteering are clear. As an anti-war novel, too, its message could hardly be clearer.

All Quiet on the Western Front Does Not Include an Effective Pacifist Politics

Elisabeth Krimmer

Elisabeth Krimmer is chair of the Russian Program and an undergraduate adviser in German at the University of California, Davis.

In the following selection, Krimmer argues that All Quiet on the Western Front *is obsessed with bodily functions, wounds, and the effect of war on bodies. She says that Erich Maria Remarque also presents his characters as victims who are traumatized and damaged by war. She asserts that Remarque's characters—as bodies or victims—have little agency or ability to act. As a result, according to Krimmer, the novel does not allow for any effective action against war or on behalf of peace. Thus, while it is antiwar, she suggests, it is so in a politically ineffective way.*

Several critics have attempted to disparage [Erich Maria] Remarque, the infamous author of an essay on cocktails, with references to his riches, his hedonistic lifestyle, and his appreciation for creaturely comforts including good food and alcohol. It is certainly true that some of his works exhibit a fascination with the exhilaration of car races, the glamour of Monte Carlo, oysters, and Chateau Lafite [an expensive wine], but references of this kind are outweighed by far by Remarque's obsession with "the body in pain." His novels are filled with descriptions of torture and mutilation, of maimed and wounded bodies, of suffering, pain, and death. *Der Funke*

Elisabeth Krimmer, "7: War and the Body: Remarque," *The Representation of War in German Literature: From 1800 to the Present*, New York: Cambridge University Press, 2010, pp. 95–98. Copyright © 2010 by Cambridge University Press. All rights reserved. Reproduced by permission.

Leben (The Spark of Life, 1952), for example, Remarque's depiction of life in a Nazi concentration camp, details the effects of crippling violence and torture on the whole of the human body. *Zeit zu leben und Zeit zu sterben* (A Time to Live and a Time to Die, 1954), his Second World War novel about the horrors and crimes on the Eastern front, opens with a grueling description of the putrefaction and decomposition of dead soldiers in thawing ice and snow. *Im Westen nichts Neues* [*All Quiet on the Western Front*] contains horrifying accounts of the debilitating injuries incurred during battle and of the many atrocious ways of dying in combat. Bodies keep running even after their heads have been torn off. They run without feet on splintering stumps. Severed hands, arms, and legs are strewn across the battlefield. Soldiers kill their opponents by splitting their faces with spades. There are soldiers without arms, without legs, without chins, without faces. This focus on bodily injury is uniquely suited to convey the terror of the First World War, which far surpassed previous wars not only in terms of casualty numbers, but also, as [Joanna] Bourke explains, "led to amputations on a scale never seen before, or since."

Bodies and Wounds

Even when he does not focus on wounds and injuries, Remarque's attentiveness to the body and its functions is paramount. Both the intake of food and the passing out of excrements occupy center-stage: "Dem Soldaten ist sein Magen und seine Verdauung ein vertrauteres Gebiet als jedem anderen Menschen" (The soldier is more familiar with his stomach and digestion than every other human being). Numerous metaphors are taken from the realm of nutrition: the division cook is a tomato head, private Tjaden is a herring, and artillery fire is "dicke Brocken" (big crumbs). The narrative of Paul Bäumer creates an economy of war in which different bodily states and functions become interchangeable. Death is converted into food, e.g., more food for the survivors who get the rations of their dead comrades, and food is converted into sexuality, e.g., when bread is used as payment for sexual favors. Remarque expounds on the life of the latrines, on Private Tjaden's habit of bed wetting, on the details of delousing, the effects of fear on one's bowels and of sleep deprivation on the body. Throughout his novel, Remarque lets the body talk. Fear and courage, instincts and responses on the battlefield are direct emanations of the body that circumvent the control of the conscious mind: "in unserm Blut [ist] ein Kontakt angeknipst" (in our blood a conduit has been switched on). *Im Westen nichts Neues* stands out not because it portrays gruesome wounds but because it recreates the sheer physicality of warfare in its many facets. Even Henri Barbusse, whose *Under Fire* paints the misery of a mud-drenched existence in the trenches in drastic detail, cannot rival Remarque's images of bodily abjection or his vast repertoire of body functions.

Undoubtedly, Remarque's focus on the body and its pain conveys a drastic critique of war. Remarque's body talk offers a radical counter-narrative to the notion of war as spiritual reawakening that dominated the war discourse of the political right. In *Im Westen*, death and injury are not moments of national rejuvenation but instances of personal loss. Remarque does not embrace the stab-in-the-back legend or the idea of regeneration through violence. And yet, in spite of its critical impetus, Remarque manages to embed his narrative of the body in pain in a consoling context. In almost Homeric [after the ancient Greek epic poet Homer] fashion, Remarque combines the description of wounds with stories and telltale details that use the moment of death to introduce images of pulsing life: there is a young recruit, who shits his pants and whose body is identified because of its missing underwear. There is the dying Kemmerich, who worries about his stolen watch and whose mother cried incessantly when she took her son to the train station. The stylistic simplicity of these scenes, the absence of irony, the focus on the narrator's compassion for his comrades help to situate the wounded and dying in a context of friendship and family. This exclusive focus on the most basic human relationships restores dignity to the victims, but it also stands in stark contrast to the anonymity of mass death in the wastelands of the First World War. While the most famous war memorials, such as Sir Edwin Lutyens's Cenotaph in London or his Memorial to the Missing at Thiepval on the Somme, are dedicated to the unknown soldier of the First World War, *Im Westen nichts Neues* celebrates individuality. It is precisely because Remarque's novel reverses and obfuscates the identity-erasing murderousness of the First World War, where up to half of those killed were unidentified, that it is able to illustrate the magnitude and futility of every individual's pain and loss. As the trauma of anonymous slaughter gives way to the commemoration of individual destinies, the novel again combines the depiction of suffering and loss with an offer of comfort and a confirmation of meaning.

Agency Even After Death

Throughout the novel, the notion of the pure body has an equalizing potential. Paul and his comrades do not bear the imprint of any particular political party, and even social class is erased when Private Tjaden realizes that "ein Kaiser auch genauso zur Latrine muß wie ich" (an Emperor has to use the latrine same as I do). On the other hand, while the pure body is essentially democratic, it does not carry the potential of agency. Significantly, it is in the moment of death that Remarque's concept of the pure and autonomous body achieves culmination. When a soldier is dying, his body takes complete control: "Das Fleisch zerschmilzt, die Stirn wölbt sich stärker, die Backenknochen stehen vor. Das Skelett arbeitet sich durch" (The flesh melts, the forehead is raised in a more forceful arch, the cheek bones protrude. The skeleton presses to the surface). In the process of decomposition when fingernails and hair keep growing, the body becomes a subject in its own right. "Die Tage sind heiβ, und die Toten liegen unbeerdigt ... Manchen treiben die Bäuche auf wie Ballons. Sie zischen, rülpsen und bewegen sich. Das Gas rumort in ihnen" (The days are hot, and the dead lie about unburied ... The stomachs of some rise like balloons. They hiss, burp and move. Gas rumbles inside them). Since Remarque's soldiers are reduced to the body, they achieve agency only when they decompose.

In the *Body in Pain*, Elaine Scarry speaks of the reality-conferring power of the wounded body. According to Scarry, the hurt body is both referentially unstable and indisputably real. Because it has no inherent meaning, the "compelling and vivid reality" of the wounded body can be used to confer legitimacy onto immaterial ideas and "become an attribute of an issue that at that moment has no independent reality." Dead bodies are not stable signs, and pure bodies are not political agents. Because Remarque's soldiers are reduced to a physical existence, they are victims of politics, but never political agents. Since Remarque's representation of the body in pain is paired with an elaborate victim discourse that encompasses all aspects of the soldier's existence, it cannot form the foundation of a fight for peace, which must be built on notions of agency. While Remarque's focus on the body in pain constitutes a powerful anti-war discourse, it cannot move beyond critique toward a politics of peace.

In his biting essay "Hat Erich Maria Remarque wirklich gelebt?" (Did Erich Maria Remarque really exist?), Mynona, aka Salomo Friedlaender, calls Remarque the "Chaplin of German philosophy." Unlike Vera Brittain and Henri Barbusse, who place their hopes in socialism and political activism, *Im Westen nichts Neues* does not present a coherent theory of the social and political factors that lead to war nor does it offer any guidance as to how to prevent future wars. Remarque's protagonist evinces a conscious abstention from historical reflection that is facilitated by the resistance of the Great War itself to straightforward explanations and narratives. Consequently, Paul Bäumer's declared intent to fight "gegen dieses, das uns beide zerschlug" (against that which shattered both of us) and his desperate cry that all soldiers are going to march "gegen wen, gegen wen?" (against whom, against whom), though meant to signal determination, are also indicative of helplessness and lack of direction. Significantly, the narrator Paul is portrayed as a victim, and his youth, his lack of experience, truncated education, and the fact that Paul and his comrades occupy the very bottom of the military hierarchy, only serve to reinforce this role. Remarque's emphasis on his narrator's youth and victimization are designed to lend particular power and urgency to his critique of war, but they also deprive his protagonist of any prospect of effective resistance. Paul's victim status allows for a certain ambiguity. On the one hand, *Im Westen nichts Neues* might be said to showcase Paul Bäumer's helplessness in order to incite action in its readers. In other words, by introducing a naïve protagonist, Remarque calls on his readers to finish the thoughts that Paul Bäumer could not afford to develop during his short life in the trenches. But it is also possible that the novel invites readers to share Paul's sense of victimization and thus confers legitimacy on resigned inaction.

All Quiet on the Western Front Is a Work of Radicalism, Not Pacifism

Gregor Dallas

Gregor Dallas is a British historian and the author of Poisoned Peace: 1945, The War That Never Ended.

In the following article, Dallas argues that the Allies saw in All Quiet on the Western Front *a plea for universal brotherhood and pacifism but that in Germany,* All Quiet *was seen as a rejection of the old Germany, which had lost the war. Dallas points out that* All Quiet *does not acknowledge German aggression and does not envision an end to the war. He concludes that the rejection of the past, the unwillingness to accept guilt, and the failure to imagine a future all pointed to Germany's ongoing radicalism and militarism. Thus Dallas sees* All Quiet *as looking toward the Second World War.*

We all wept at the end of Erich Maria Remarque's *All Quiet on the Western Front*. We were scandalized by young Paul Bäumer's death: just weeks before the Armistice, he sank under a sniper's bullet. Yes, we all wept. But were all those tears shed for the same reason?

Pacifism and Disillusionment

Paul and his comrades were Germans. For British, French and American readers, Remarque had made the absurdity of war universal; surely they thought, when the book was published in 1929, this was proof that an international understanding was possible. There were those poignant scenes between enemies, as when Paul lay in a shell crater with a Frenchman he had killed with his own hands. 'Forgive me, *camarade!* We always realize too late,' he cries out from his muddy hole. 'Why don't they keep on reminding us that you are all miserable wretches just like us?' Or, again, the sight of the Russian prisoners of war; Paul finds them more brotherly than his own people. Or the human wrecks in a military hospital: 'there are hundreds of thousands of them in Germany, hundreds of thousands of them in France, hundred of thousands of them in Russia.'

Who had caused all this? The older generation, said Paul and his comrades: 'While they went on writing and making speeches, we saw field hospitals and men dying.'

The gulf that the war opened between generations seemed to be the experience of all countries. It was most graphically represented by the barrier that separated older civilians at 'home' from young soldiers on the war front—there was no communication between them. When Paul travelled home on the leave he crossed 'the boundaries of my youth'. At home he could not talk about the front; he had to lie to his own dying mother. Even one year's distance in age could make a difference.

Paul and his comrades, on encountering fresh young recruits, felt old, as if they had been 'in the army for a thousand years.'

Pacifism, disillusionment and the derangement of the 'lost generation' were often taken as the central themes of Remarque's novel. That was what moved a whole new generation in the 1960s—for western youth then also considered themselves a pacifist, 'lost generation'. As the 'generation gap' widened the novel seemed increasingly relevant: Remarque came to be seen not only as the spokesman of peace in his time, but also a prophet.

Different Tears

Remarque had certainly earned the sympathy of the West. Copies of *All Quiet on the Western Front* fed the same bonfire in Berlin as the books of Thomas Mann, Albert Einstein, James Joyce and Ernest Hemingway; its author was forced into exile; his sister was beheaded during the Second World War. But *All Quiet on the Western Front* had, before all this happened, been a bestseller in Germany and the Germans had also wept—but not with the same tears as the British and the French.

Germany was different. There are little details in the novel suggesting that the Kaiser's Reich was not the same kind of belligerent as the Western Allies. For example, Paul and his company are 'sent out to evacuate a district'—the Western Allies did not evacuate whole districts as the Germans did in occupied Belgium and northern France. On their way out the company meets the 'escaping' locals: 'their figures are bowed, their faces full of misery, despair, haste and resignation'— under the Hindenburg Programme of 1916–17 tens of thousands of Belgian and French civilians were shipped by cattle trains to labour in German factories. There is discussion in Paul's hometown about Germany's planned annexations—no other belligerent had such vast territorial ambitions as the German Reich. There are the Russian prisoners-of-war: 'their backs and their heads are bowed. Their knees bent, they look up at you with their heads on one side when they stick their hands out and beg . . . '—Remarque is describing inmates of a concentration camp.

But most notably, Remarque's account of a 'generation that was destroyed by the war' differs in several important ways from the Western depictions of the 'lost generation'. In the first place, it completely cuts itself from its roots. This is not the case in English or French war literature. [Poet and novelist] Siegfried Sassoon and his soldiers, for instance, still guard strong memories and images of England, [novelist]

Henri Barbusse's troops are merely French peasants on the front; Paul and his German comrades are unsparing in their violence against the older generation and civilians. Corporal Himmelstoss is tied up in a quilt cover and beaten into a gutter—he gave 'a wonderful, high-pitched shriek that soon got cut off.' Paul's former schoolmaster is forced to compete in drill with the old school janitor; the schoolmaster scurries back and forth 'like a stuck pig', his 'panting is music to our ears.' Glass bottles are thrown at the hospital nuns who are chanting a prayer. Thirdly, earlier education is abandoned; all 'the rubbish, the stuff they fill our head with' is cast aside— the 'first shell to land went straight for our hearts . . . ; we believe in the war.' Finally, there is a specific kind of isolation described in Remarque's novel, such as the young, raving recruit who 'collapsed in on himself like a tree that is rotten inside'; and there is the case of Paul's own isolation towards the end of the novel.

Violence and Fanaticism

It was violence and fanaticism that made Paul Bäumer's generation so special. In the two decades before the First World War there developed in Germany radical youth movements— like the *Wandervögel*—that had no parallel in the West. During the war they merged with a cult of the soldier which, again, was never witnessed in France, Britain or America. Understandably, after 1918 Westerners, having experienced the horror of the war, called peace and reconciliation—they wept when they recognized the message in *All Quiet on the Western Front*. It was not the same in Germany.

'Haie, what would you do if the war ended?' asks Muller, who before the war had been a star pupil of physics. Paul interrupts and tells Haie to kick Müller's 'arse from here to kingdom come for talking about that sort of thing here.' But the question of the war's end never goes away. Later Paul reflects that 'we shall march forward' with 'our dead comrades

Kat (Louis Wolheim), left, serves as a mentor and friend to Paul Bäumer (Lew Ayres), right, in the 1930 film version of All Quiet on the Western Front. *Kat later dies, a loss which deeply affects Paul.* © Bettmann/Corbis.

beside us . . . but against whom?' Here, in a pure and unadulterated form, is the German cult of the soldier—and Germany wept. Germans and westerners indeed wept together, but they were not weeping for the same reason. Paul's death was a blood sacrifice. 'I stand up, I am very calm. Let the months come, and the years, they'll take nothing more from me . . . As long as life is there it will make its own way.'

There is a hint, towards the end of the novel, that the war would never end. And, indeed, the war did not end for Germany on 11 November 1918; it simply marched east. Germans were still fighting Poles in Silesia in 1921. Volunteer corps were fighting the Bolsheviks in the Baltic States. Within Germany the war, like Remarque's new recruit, 'collapsed in on itself.' Soldiers fought soldiers; in Berlin the new civil war fought between soldiers from the trenches and sailors from the rear (the *Etappe*)—Germany's own peculiar version of tension between the front and home. [Adolf] Hitler's storm troopers were born out of this.

'Summer, 1918,' exclaims Paul as he nears his own end. 'A wind of hope sweeping over the burnt-out fields . . . ' Perhaps, he reflects, the British and the Americans have the greater forces, but 'we haven't been defeated, because as soldiers we are better and more experienced.' That is why Germany wept on reading *All Quiet on the Western Front*: the fight, and the sacrifice, had not yet been concluded.

The failure of the West's hopeful statesmen to detect the difference between Western and German tears was one of the main causes of a Second World War. The warning to our times is obvious: some 'universal truths' are not as universal as we would like.

All Quiet on the Western Front Offers a Political Critique of Modernity and Modern Warfare

Stuart A. Scheingold

Stuart A. Scheingold is emeritus professor of political science at the University of Washington.

In the following selection, Scheingold argues that All Quiet on the Western Front *criticizes modernity through its view of modern warfare. Erich Maria Remarque sees war as dehumanizing, Scheingold says, and connects this dehumanization in part to technological advances and achievements.* All Quiet *chronicles the irony of great technological achievements used to kill. In particular, Scheingold asserts, Remarque criticizes surgeons and doctors whose professional skills are used on behalf of war rather than for healing; thus,* All Quiet *shows the oppressive nature of modernity's technological advances.*

Erich Maria Remarque's soldier's-eye view of World War I contrasts dramatically with [Ernest] Hemingway's *A Farewell to Arms.* The bulk of the novel details the many horrors of the foot soldiers' war in the trenches on the Western Front. Remarque's dominant message is simply that war is hell—almost literally so. But there are also two accompanying messages of betrayal, which identify the self-serving warmongering of the economic and military elites and the false promises of the modern project. Taken together, these latter

Stuart A. Scheingold, "Anti-War Novels in the Twentieth Century: The Road to Late Modernity," *The Political Novel: Re-Imagining the Twentieth Century*, New York: Continuum International Publishing Group, 2010, pp. 30–32. Copyright © 2010 by Stuart A. Scheingold. All rights reserved. Reproduced by Permission.

messages strike populist and anti-modernist notes, in which progress and war emerge as a conspiracy against rank and file workers and soldiers.

Comradeship and Alienation

Insofar as the experience of war has any redemptive benefit, it would seem to be in the salt-of-the-earth solidarity among comrades and, to an extent, between combatants and the enemy. "Comradeship" and "*esprit de corps*" are, according to the narrator Paul Baumer, "in the field developed into the finest thing that arose from the war."

> We sit opposite one another, Kat and I, two soldiers in shabby coats, cooking a goose in the middle of the night. We don't talk much, but I believe we have a more complete community with one another than even lovers have.

Paul takes solace from his comrades' voices, which are "the strongest most comforting thing there is anywhere."

Because this is the solidarity of collective dehumanization it provides cold comfort. The dehumanization begins with military training which, as Paul puts it, makes them "hard, suspicious, pitiless, vicious, tough—and that was good; for these attributes were just what we lacked." Then, there are the squalid living conditions in the trenches where the "repulsive" rats are "so fat—the kind we call corpse rats." The soldiers are in constant fear for their lives while witnessing the pain, the suffering and the death of their comrades. "We have become wild beasts. We do not fight, we defend ourselves against annihilation." However, in becoming wild beasts so as to avoid physical annihilation, they are, Remarque reveals, spiritually and emotionally annihilated—resulting in an alienation from society and from self.

The annihilation is particularly devastating for "the young men of twenty" who have been robbed of their youth and their futures. They are without the older men's insulation of the everyday: "wives, children, occupations, and interests . . . that the war can not obliterate . . . We young men of twenty . . . have only our parents, and some, perhaps, a girl—that is not much, for at our age the influence of parents is at its weakest and girls have not yet got a hold over us." When he returns home on leave, he finds himself completely at odds with civilians, including a home-front major who chastises him for not saluting: "You think you can bring your front-line manners here, what? . . . Thank God, we still have discipline here!" But he also finds himself estranged from the family and friends for whom he is fighting. "They talk too much for me. They have worries, aims, desires, that I cannot comprehend."

> [T]he things and events of our existence . . . cut us off and made the world of our parents incomprehensible to us—for then we surrendered ourselves to events and were lost in them, and the least little thing was enough to carry us down the stream of eternity.

Paul's estrangement radiates inward to his own life. "All I do know is that this business about professions and studies and salaries and so on—it makes me sick, it is and always was disgusting. I don't see anything at all."

Estrangement and Dehumanization

Being at home is revealing but dreadfully so. "I ought never to have come here. Out there I was indifferent and often hopeless—I will never be able to be so again. I was a soldier, and now I am nothing but an agony for myself, for my mother, for everything that is so comfortless and without end." "But now I see that I have been crushed without knowing it, I find I do not belong here any more, it is a foreign world."

While the novel is, then, dominated by a searing and straightforward account of the dehumanization of trench warfare, there is also an unmistakable awareness of the contradictions of the modern project. War is seen as bending technological achievements to its own destructive purposes—with

Like the novel, the 1930 film adaptation of All Quiet on the Western Front *shows how dehumanizing trench warfare was during World War I.* © John Springer Collection/Corbis.

flamethrowers, improved tanks and airplanes offered as cases in point. Attention is called to the way that airplanes serve as artillery spotters and thus become agents of sudden death from distant and unseen big guns. Paul observes bitterly that for war, "the keenest brains of the world invent weapons and words to make it yet more refined and enduring."

Medical knowledge and the medical profession are similarly disparaged. Early on, mention is made of "splendid artificial limbs," which as everyone knows are not splendid. And the hospital is both a testimonial to the ravages of war and a laboratory for mobilizing medical support of war making.

> A man can stop a bullet and be killed; he can get wounded, and the hospital is the next stop. There, if they do not amputate him, he sooner or later falls into the hands of one of those staff surgeons who, with the War Service Cross in his

button-hole, says to him: "What, one leg a bit short? If you have any pluck you don't need to run at the front. The man is A1. Dismiss!"

Profit from War

The surgeon serves both his military masters and himself because: "What he wants is little dogs to experiment with, so the war is a glorious time for him, as it is for all surgeons." What then of so-called civilization? "It must all be lies and of no account when the culture of a thousand years could not prevent this stream of blood being poured out, these torture-chambers in their hundreds of thousands. A hospital alone shows what war is."

Towards the end of the book the overtly political themes are introduced, again prompted by Paul's home leave. He becomes aware of the contrast between the squandering of resources through war profiteering and military incompetence and the ever more desperate lot of the soldiers in the trenches and the poor at home. "The factory owners in Germany have grown wealthy;—dysentery dissolves our bowels." With respect to his mother's cancer operation, he observes that poor people need operations that they fear they cannot afford. Yet they "don't dare to ask the price," because they also fear that "the surgeon might take it amiss." "And generals too," adds [Paul's comrade] Detering, "they become famous through war . . . There are other people behind there who profit by the war, that's certain."

All Quiet on the Western Front Shows War as Destructively Masculine

Mary Warner

Mary Warner is associate professor of English at San Jose State University in California.

In the following essay, Warner argues that in All Quiet on the Western Front, *the war is presented as an assault on the feminine. She says that the boys who go off to the front are forced to kill all the softness within them, such as tenderness and childhood friendships. She asserts that Erich Maria Remarque presents the soldiers as yearning for, or attracted to, the comfort of mothers, which they must leave behind when they go to the front. Warner concludes that questions about gender and the military remain politically important today. She argues that one of the great tragedies of war is that it destroys the human spirit.*

In the epigraph [to *All Quiet on the Western Front*] the author suggests that "[the book] will try simply to tell of a generation of men who, even though they may have escaped shells, were destroyed by the war." [Erich Maria] Remarque alludes here specifically to the destruction that permeates the spirit of this generation of men who fought in World War I. Certainly, the human spirit must be described as including the capacity for compassion, sensitivity, and other life-affirming feelings. In casting sensitive poet Paul Bäumer as narrator, Remarque exposes the successful war against the feminine that was and is part of any military campaign.

Mary Warner, "The War Against the Feminine: Erich Maria Remarque's *All Quiet on the Western Front* (1929)," *Women in Literature: Reading Through the Lens of Gender,* edited by Jerilyn Fisher and Ellen S. Silber, Westport, CT: Greenwood Press, ABC-CLIO, 2003, pp. 4–6. Copyright © 2003 by Jerilyn Fisher and Ellen S. Silber. All rights reserved. Reproduced by Permission.

The Iron Youth

Paul and his classmates, enlisting at eighteen, had been labeled by their teacher as the "Iron Youth"; however, they find in the first terrifying, disillusioning moments at the Front that they are neither "iron" (unfeeling and invulnerable) nor are they any longer youth. Combat and glorification of the "Fatherland" impel Paul and his young peers not only to fight for their lives and their country but also to battle an interior war against their "feminine" sides in order to triumph in physical battle.

The opening chapter highlights several ways the feminine spirit is crushed. Speaking of Kantorek, schoolmaster and proponent of the male-oriented world, Paul says: "He was about the same size as Corporal Himmelstoss, the 'terror of Klosterberg.' It is queer that the unhappiness of the world is so often brought on by small men." Paul's observation raises interesting questions for the classroom about the pressure boys and men experience to appear strong, and the ways that they sometimes "compensate" for having short stature or slight build in a culture still saturated with tall, muscular, agile prototypes for male success. Kantorek, indeed, suggests such "compensation" in his being no less than a martinet, indoctrinating Paul and his schoolmates about the honor of enlisting; the schoolmaster's "long lectures" continue until all the boys enlist, including Joseph Behm, a "plump, homely fellow." Paul's description of Behm associates him with the stereotypically feminine: He is less athletic and therefore less "soldier-like" than the other boys; he enlists to avoid ostracization by his peers, and tragically, though perhaps inevitably, he is the first to fall in battle. And there can be no tears shed by any of the "spirit scarred" remnant.

Remarque devotes extensive text to those dying and to the guilt of the living young soldiers. When Kemmerich dies, Paul

In this film still from the 1930 adaptation of All Quiet on the Western Front, *schoolboys, including protagonist Paul Bäumer, at right, enjoy a brief rest from the war.* © Hulton Archive/Moviepix/Getty Images.

faces the greatest pathos, having come from Kemmerich's hometown, and he is haunted by the image of Kemmerich's mother, "a good plump matron," crying as she implored Paul to

> look after Franz. . . . Indeed he did have the face like a child, and such frail bones that after four weeks' pack-carrying he already had flat feet. But how can a man look after everyone in the field.

The male "ironness" must dominate; there is no "looking after" others, even one's comrades. Paul cannot allow his friend's softness to pierce the soldier's shield of stoicism for more than a few seconds. Just outside the dead man's hospital room, he reluctantly gives away Franz Kemmerich's boots, seeming to give away with them much of his anger and grief at losing his childhood playmate.

Mothers vs. Fantasies

Paul experiences his helplessness here and indeed, there is no haven from heartless, dehumanizing conditions at the front. But his earlier description of Kemmerich's mother (which mirrors that of other mothers in the text) portrays the maternal as physically ample—capable, in absentia, of providing images of comfort. Symbolically, Paul's lengthy descriptions of shelling further illuminate the consolation that mothers and, by extension, Mother Earth provides:

> To no man does the earth mean so much as to the soldier. When he presses himself down upon her long and powerfully, when he buries his face and his limbs deep into her for fear of death by shell-fire, then she is his only friend, his brother, his mother; he stifles his terror and his cries in her silence and her security; she shelters him and releases him.

The comforting aspect of maternal imagery looms in dynamic comparison/contrast with the poster girl who mesmerizes the battle-dirtied, sexually deprived males. The poster image comforts too, but is too delicate and sensuous to be life sustaining. Yet, like the other sexual symbols in the text (the women with whom Paul and others have brief sexual encounters and the women that officers "get"), the poster girl offers the soldiers affirmation of their maleness so necessary to their survival. Paul and his companions fantasize about sexuality to avoid emotional breakdown, which would be their demise in facing the physically brutal reality of war.

Repression of the Feminine

Only those soldiers who have repressed the feminine can survive in the masculine frontlines. Paul labels recruits "infants": They come to the front less hardened; they weep; they are innocent to the potency of shelling; they hold to the delicacy of their civilian youth. To Paul, they are childlike and thus feminized by cultural standards.

It brings a lump into the throat to see how they go over, run and fall ... a man would like to spank them ... they have no business to be [here] ... their shoulders are too narrow, their bodies too slight.

Herein lies the greatest irony in the war against the feminine. On one of the days when the masculine war world is described as "quiet," when Paul feels free to release some of his ironness, he is killed.

All Quiet on the Western Front provides the opportunity to examine the military and the role of women in armed forces. Contemporary students are not far removed from controversies over females enrolling at the Citadel [a military college in South Carolina], or from claims of sexual harassment by female or homosexual officers. Also: How do qualities of the feminine and masculine relate in military training? Are both welcomed? In particular, Paul left at home an original play and "a bundle of poems"; what is the place of artists or of creative or sensitive personalities in war or other experiences demanding destruction? This novel, like *Red Badge of Courage*, like Hemingway's short story "Soldier's Home," and the war-movie genre, insists that readers weigh the necessity of having a strong military against the costs of war, and especially those costs that forever distort and diminish the human spirit.

Contemporary
Perspectives on War

A History of Violence

Steven Pinker

Steven Pinker is Harvard College Professor and Johnstone Family Professor of Psychology at Harvard University. He is the author of The Better Angels of Our Nature.

In the following selection, Pinker argues that violence has been declining over the course of history. He attributes this to several factors, including the formation of large, powerful states that can enforce peace, the rise of reason, the lengthening of the human lifespan by technology, the development and sharing of technology and commerce, and the expansion of people's circle of empathy as the remoter parts of the world become more accessible to each individual. Pinker does not say that these trends must or inevitably will continue, but he says that they should be recognized so that we can see what aspects of our society have made our lives better and less violent.

In sixteenth-century Paris, a popular form of entertainment was cat-burning, in which a cat was hoisted in a sling on a stage and slowly lowered into a fire. According to historian Norman Davies, "[T]he spectators, including kings and queens, shrieked with laughter as the animals, howling with pain, were singed, roasted, and finally carbonized." Today, such sadism would be unthinkable in most of the world. This change in sensibilities is just one example of perhaps the most important and most underappreciated trend in the human saga: Violence has been in decline over long stretches of history, and today we are probably living in the most peaceful moment of our species' time on earth.

Steven Pinker, "A History of Violence," *The New Republic*, March 19, 2007, pp. 18–21. Copyright © 2007 by The New Republic. All rights reserved. Reproduced by permission.

In the decade of Darfur and Iraq, and shortly after the century of Stalin, Hitler, and Mao, the claim that violence has been diminishing may seem somewhere between hallucinatory and obscene. Yet recent studies that seek to quantify the historical ebb and flow of violence point to exactly that conclusion.

Some of the evidence has been under our nose all along. Conventional history has long shown that, in many ways, we have been getting kinder and gentler. Cruelty as entertainment, human sacrifice to indulge superstition, slavery as a labor-saving device, conquest as the mission statement of government, genocide as a means of acquiring real estate, torture and mutilation as routine punishment, the death penalty for misdemeanors and differences of opinion, assassination as the mechanism of political succession, rape as the spoils of war, pogroms as outlets for frustration, homicide as the major form of conflict resolution—all were unexceptionable features of life for most of human history. But, today, they are rare to nonexistent in the West, far less common elsewhere than they used to be, concealed when they do occur, and widely condemned when they are brought to light.

At one time, these facts were widely appreciated. They were the source of notions like progress, civilization, and man's rise from savagery and barbarism. Recently, however, those ideas have come to sound corny, even dangerous. They seem to demonize people in other times and places, license colonial conquest and other foreign adventures, and conceal the crimes of our own societies. The doctrine of the noble savage—the idea that humans are peaceable by nature and corrupted by modern institutions—pops up frequently in the writing of public intellectuals like José Ortega y Gasset ("War is not an instinct but an invention"), Stephen Jay Gould ("Homo sapiens is not an evil or destructive species"), and Ashley Montagu ("Biological studies lend support to the ethic of universal brotherhood"). But, now that social scientists have started to count bodies in different historical periods, they have discovered that the romantic theory gets it backward: Far from causing us to become more violent, something in modernity and its cultural institutions has made us nobler.

To be sure, any attempt to document changes in violence must be soaked in uncertainty. In much of the world, the distant past was a tree falling in the forest with no one to hear it, and, even for events in the historical record, statistics are spotty until recent periods. Long-term trends can be discerned only by smoothing out zigzags and spikes of horrific bloodletting. And the choice to focus on relative rather than absolute numbers brings up the moral imponderable of whether it is worse for 50 percent of a population of 100 to be killed or 1 percent in a population of one billion.

Yet, despite these caveats, a picture is taking shape. The decline of violence is a fractal phenomenon, visible at the scale of millennia, centuries, decades, and years. It applies over several orders of magnitude of violence, from genocide to war to rioting to homicide to the treatment of children and animals. And it appears to be a worldwide trend, though not a homogeneous one. The leading edge has been in Western societies, especially England and Holland, and there seems to have been a tipping point at the onset of the Age of Reason in the early seventeenth century.

At the widest-angle view, one can see a whopping difference across the millennia that separate us from our pre-state ancestors. Contra leftist anthropologists who celebrate the noble savage, quantitative body-counts—such as the proportion of prehistoric skeletons with axemarks and embedded arrowheads or the proportion of men in a contemporary foraging tribe who die at the hands of other men—suggest that pre-state societies were far more violent than our own. It is true that raids and battles killed a tiny percentage of the numbers that die in modern warfare. But, in tribal violence, the clashes are more frequent, the percentage of men in the population who fight is greater, and the rates of death per battle are higher. According to anthropologists like Lawrence Keeley, Stephen LeBlanc, Phillip Walker, and Bruce Knauft, these factors combine to yield population-wide rates of death in tribal warfare that dwarf those of modern times. If the wars of the twentieth century had killed the same proportion of the population that die in the wars of a typical tribal society, there would have been two billion deaths, not 100 million.

Political correctness from the other end of the ideological spectrum has also distorted many people's conception of violence in early civilizations—namely, those featured in the Bible. This supposed source of moral values contains many celebrations of genocide, in which the Hebrews, egged on by God, slaughter every last resident of an invaded city. The Bible also prescribes death by stoning as the penalty for a long list of nonviolent infractions, including idolatry, blasphemy, homosexuality, adultery, disrespecting one's parents, and picking up sticks on the Sabbath. The Hebrews, of course, were no more murderous than other tribes; one also finds frequent boasts of torture and genocide in the early histories of the Hindus, Christians, Muslims, and Chinese.

At the century scale, it is hard to find quantitative studies of deaths in warfare spanning medieval and modern times. Several historians have suggested that there has been an increase in the number of recorded wars across the centuries to the present, but, as political scientist James Payne has noted, this may show only that "the Associated Press is a more comprehensive source of information about battles around the world than were sixteenth-century monks." Social histories of the West provide evidence of numerous barbaric practices that became obsolete in the last five centuries, such as slavery, amputation, blinding, branding, flaying, disembowelment, burning at the stake, breaking on the wheel, and so on. Meanwhile, for another kind of violence—homicide—the data are abundant and striking. The criminologist Manuel Eisner has as-

sembled hundreds of homicide estimates from Western European localities that kept records at some point between 1200
and the mid-1990s. In every country he analyzed, murder
rates declined steeply—for example, from 24 homicides per
100,000 Englishmen in the fourteenth century to 0.6 per
100,000 by the early 1960s.

On the scale of decades, comprehensive data again paint a
shockingly happy picture: Global violence has fallen steadily
since the middle of the twentieth century. According to the
Human Security Brief 2006, the number of battle deaths in
interstate wars has declined from more than 65,000 per year
in the 1950s to less than 2,000 per year in this decade. In
Western Europe and the Americas, the second half of the century saw a steep decline in the number of wars, military coups,
and deadly ethnic riots.

Zooming in by a further power of ten exposes yet another
reduction. After the cold war, every part of the world saw a
steep drop-off in state-based conflicts, and those that do occur
are more likely to end in negotiated settlements rather than
being fought to the bitter end. Meanwhile, according to political scientist Barbara Harff, between 1989 and 2005 the number of campaigns of mass killing of civilians decreased by 90
percent.

The decline of killing and cruelty poses several challenges
to our ability to make sense of the world. To begin with, how
could so many people be so wrong about something so important? Partly, it's because of a cognitive illusion: We estimate
the probability of an event from how easy it is to recall examples. Scenes of carnage are more likely to be relayed to our
living rooms and burned into our memories than footage of
people dying of old age. Partly, it's an intellectual culture that
is loath to admit that there could be anything good about the
institutions of civilization and Western society. Partly, it's the
incentive structure of the activism and opinion markets: No
one ever attracted followers and donations by announcing

that things keep getting better. And part of the explanation lies in the phenomenon itself. The decline of violent behavior has been paralleled by a decline in attitudes that tolerate or glorify violence, and often the attitudes are in the lead. As deplorable as they are, the abuses at Abu Ghraib and the lethal injections of a few murderers in Texas are mild by the standards of atrocities in human history. But, from a contemporary vantage point, we see them as signs of how low our behavior can sink, not of how high our standards have risen.

The other major challenge posed by the decline of violence is how to explain it. A force that pushes in the same direction across many epochs, continents, and scales of social organization mocks our standard tools of causal explanation. The usual suspects—guns, drugs, the press, American culture—aren't nearly up to the job. Nor could it possibly be explained by evolution in the biologist's sense: Even if the meek could inherit the earth, natural selection could not favor the genes for meekness quickly enough. In any case, human nature has not changed so much as to have lost its taste for violence. Social psychologists find that at least 80 percent of people have fantasized about killing someone they don't like. And modern humans still take pleasure in viewing violence, if we are to judge by the popularity of murder mysteries, Shakespearean dramas, Mel Gibson movies, video games, and hockey.

What *has* changed, of course, is people's willingness to act on these fantasies. The sociologist Norbert Elias suggested that European modernity accelerated a "civilizing process" marked by increases in self-control, long-term planning, and sensitivity to the thoughts and feelings of others. These are precisely the functions that today's cognitive neuroscientists attribute to the prefrontal cortex. But this only raises the question of why humans have increasingly exercised that part of their brains. No one knows why our behavior has come under the control of the better angels of our nature, but there are four plausible suggestions.

The first is that Hobbes got it right. Life in a state of nature is nasty, brutish, and short, not because of a primal thirst for blood but because of the inescapable logic of anarchy. Any beings with a modicum of self-interest may be tempted to invade their neighbors to steal their resources. The resulting fear of attack will tempt the neighbors to strike first in preemptive self-defense, which will in turn tempt the first group to strike against them preemptively, and so on. This danger can be defused by a policy of deterrence—don't strike first, retaliate if struck—but, to guarantee its credibility, parties must avenge all insults and settle all scores, leading to cycles of bloody vendetta. These tragedies can be averted by a state with a monopoly on violence, because it can inflict disinterested penalties that eliminate the incentives for aggression, thereby defusing anxieties about preemptive attack and obviating the need to maintain a hair-trigger propensity for retaliation. Indeed, Eisner and Elias attribute the decline in European homicide to the transition from knightly warrior societies to the centralized governments of early modernity. And, today, violence continues to fester in zones of anarchy, such as frontier regions, failed states, collapsed empires, and territories contested by mafias, gangs, and other dealers of contraband.

Payne suggests another possibility: that the critical variable in the indulgence of violence is an overarching sense that life is cheap. When pain and early death are everyday features of one's own life, one feels fewer compunctions about inflicting them on others. As technology and economic efficiency lengthen and improve our lives, we place a higher value on life in general.

A third theory, championed by Robert Wright, invokes the logic of non-zero-sum games: scenarios in which two agents can each come out ahead if they cooperate, such as trading goods, dividing up labor, or sharing the peace dividend that comes from laying down their arms. As people acquire knowhow that they can share cheaply with others and develop technologies that allow them to spread their goods and ideas over larger territories at lower cost, their incentive to cooperate steadily increases, because other people become more valuable alive than dead.

Then there is the scenario sketched by philosopher Peter Singer. Evolution, he suggests, bequeathed people a small kernel of empathy, which by default they apply only within a narrow circle of friends and relations. Over the millennia, people's moral circles have expanded to encompass larger and larger polities: the clan, the tribe, the nation, both sexes, other races, and even animals. The circle may have been pushed outward by expanding networks of reciprocity, à la Wright, but it might also be inflated by the inexorable logic of the golden rule: The more one knows and thinks about other living things, the harder it is to privilege one's own interests over theirs. The empathy escalator may also be powered by cosmopolitanism, in which journalism, memoir, and realistic fiction make the inner lives of other people, and the contingent nature of one's own station, more palpable—the feeling that "there but for fortune go I".

Whatever its causes, the decline of violence has profound implications. It is not a license for complacency: We enjoy the peace we find today because people in past generations were appalled by the violence in their time and worked to end it, and so we should work to end the appalling violence in our time. Nor is it necessarily grounds for optimism about the immediate future, since the world has never before had national leaders who combine pre-modern sensibilities with modern weapons.

But the phenomenon does force us to rethink our understanding of violence. Man's inhumanity to man has long been a subject for moralization. With the knowledge that something has driven it dramatically down, we can also treat it as a matter of cause and effect. Instead of asking, "Why is there war?" we might ask, "Why is there peace?" From the likelihood that states will commit genocide to the way that people treat cats, we must have been doing something right. And it would be nice to know what, exactly, it is.

Seven Reasons Why We Can't Stop Making War

William J. Astore

William J. Astore is a retired lieutenant colonel.

In the following article, Astore discusses seven reasons why the world can't stop making war. He contends that the one quality that characterizes war today is endurance—it never seems to end. Among the reasons Astore lists for the world waging war, is that we've already dedicated so many of our resources to the cause of war. Astore concludes his article with seven "caps" in order to combat the seven reasons for making war.

If one quality characterizes our wars today, it's their endurance. They never seem to end.

Though war itself may not be an American inevitability, these days many factors combine to make constant war an American near certainty. Put metaphorically, our nation's pursuit of war taps so many wellsprings of our behavior that a concerted effort to cap it would dwarf BP's efforts in the Gulf of Mexico.

Our political leaders, the media, and the military interpret enduring war as a measure of our national fitness, our global power, our grit in the face of eternal danger, and our seriousness. A desire to de-escalate and withdraw, on the other hand, is invariably seen as cut-and-run appeasement and discounted as weakness. Withdrawal options are, in a pet phrase of Washington elites, invariably "off the table" when global policy is at stake, as was true during the Obama administration's full-scale reconsideration of the Afghan war in the fall of 2009.

William J. Astore, "Seven Reasons Why We Can't Stop Making War," CBSNews.com, July 9, 2010. Reprinted with permission from TomDispatch. All rights reserved. Reproduced by permission.

Viewed in this light, the president's ultimate decision to surge in Afghanistan was not only predictable, but the only course considered suitable for an American war leader. Rather than the tough choice, it was the path of least resistance.

Why do our elites so readily and regularly give war, not peace, a chance? What exactly are the wellsprings of Washington's (and America's) behavior when it comes to war and preparations for more of the same?

Consider these seven:

1. We wage war because we think we're good at it—and because, at a gut level, we've come to believe that American wars can bring good to others (hence our feel-good names for them, like Operations Enduring Freedom and Iraqi Freedom). Most Americans are not only convinced we have the best troops, the best training, and the most advanced weapons, but also the purest motives. Unlike the bad guys and the barbarians out there in the global marketplace of death, our warriors and warfighters are seen as gift-givers and freedom-bringers, not as death-dealers and resource-exploiters. Our illusions about the military we "support" serve as catalyst for, and apology for, the persistent war-making we condone.

2. We wage war because we've already devoted so many of our resources to it. It's what we're most prepared to do. More than half of discretionary federal spending goes to fund our military and its war making or war preparations. The military-industrial complex is a well-oiled, extremely profitable machine and the armed forces, our favorite child, the one we've lavished the most resources and praise upon. It's natural to give your favorite child free rein.

3. We've managed to isolate war's physical and emotional costs, leaving them on the shoulders of a tiny minority of Americans. By eliminating the draft and relying ever more on for-profit private military contractors, we've made war

a distant abstraction for most Americans, who can choose to consume it as spectacle or simply tune it out as so much background noise.

4. While war and its costs have, to date, been kept at arm's length, American society has been militarizing fast. Our media outlets, intelligence agencies, politicians, foreign policy establishment, and "homeland security" bureaucracy are so intertwined with military priorities and agendas as to be inseparable from them. In militarized America, griping about soft-hearted tactics or the outspokenness of a certain general may be tolerated, but forceful criticism of our military or our wars is still treated as deviant and "un-American."

5. Our profligate, high-tech approach to war, including those Predator and Reaper drones armed with Hellfire missiles, has served to limit American casualties—and so has limited the anger over, and harsh questioning of, our wars that might go with them. While the U.S. has had more than 1,000 troops killed in Afghanistan, over a similar period in Vietnam we lost more than 58,000 troops. Improved medical evacuation and trauma care, greater reliance on standoff precision weaponry and similar "force multipliers," stronger emphasis on "force protection" within American military units: all these and more have helped tamp down concern about the immeasurable and soaring costs of our wars.

6. As we incessantly develop those force-multiplying weapons to give us our "edge" (though never an edge that leads to victory), it's hardly surprising that the U.S. has come to dominate, if not quite monopolize, the global arms trade. In these years, as American jobs were outsourced or simply disappeared in the Great Recession, armaments have been one of our few growth industries. Endless war has proven endlessly profitable—not perhaps for all of us, but certainly for those in the business of war.

7. And don't forget the seductive power of beyond-worse-case, doomsday scenarios, of the prophecies of pundits and so-called experts, who regularly tell us that, bad as our wars may be, doing anything to end them would be far worse. A typical scenario goes like this: If we withdraw from Afghanistan, the government of Hamid Karzai will collapse, the Taliban will surge to victory, al-Qaeda will pour into Afghan safe havens, and Pakistan will be further destabilized, its atomic bombs falling into the hands of terrorists out to destroy Peoria and Orlando.

Such fevered nightmares, impossible to disprove, may be conjured at any moment to scare critics into silence. They are a convenient bogeyman, leaving us cowering as we send our superman military out to save us (and the world as well), while preserving our right to visit the mall and travel to Disney World without being nuked.

The truth is that no one really knows what would happen if the U.S. disengaged from Afghanistan. But we do know what's happening now, with us fully engaged: we're pursuing a war that's costing us nearly $7 billion a month that we're not winning (and that's arguably unwinnable), a war that may be increasing the chances of another 9/11, rather than decreasing them.

Capping the Wellsprings of War

Each one of these seven wellsprings feeding our enduring wars must be capped. So here are seven suggestions for the sort of "caps"—hopefully more effective than BP's flailing improvisations—we need to install:

1. Let's reject the idea that war is either admirable or good—and in the process, remind ourselves that others often see us as "the foreign fighters" and profligate war consumers who kill innocents (despite our efforts to apply deadly force in surgically precise ways reflecting "courageous restraint").

2. Let's cut defense spending now, and reduce the global "mission" that goes with it. Set a reasonable goal—a 6-8% reduction annually for the next 10 years, until levels of defense spending are at least back to where they were before 9/11—and then stick to it.

3. Let's stop privatizing war. Creating ever more profitable incentives for war was always a ludicrous idea. It's time to make war a non-profit, last-resort activity. And let's revive national service (including elective military service) for all young adults. What we need is a revived civilian conservation corps, not a new civilian "expeditionary" force.

4. Let's reverse the militarization of so many dimensions of our society. To cite one example, it's time to empower truly independent (non-embedded) journalists to cover our wars, and stop relying on retired generals and admirals who led our previous wars to be our media guides. Men who are beholden to their former service branch or the current defense contractor who employs them can hardly be trusted to be critical and unbiased guides to future conflicts.

5. Let's recognize that expensive high-tech weapons systems are not war-winners. They've kept us in the game without yielding decisive results—unless you measure "results" in terms of cost overruns and burgeoning federal budget deficits.

6. Let's retool our economy and reinvest our money, moving it out of the military-industrial complex and into strengthening our anemic system of mass transit, our crumbling infrastructure, and alternative energy technology. We need high-speed rail, safer roads and bridges, and more wind turbines, not more overpriced jet fighters.

7. Finally, let's banish nightmare scenarios from our minds. The world is scary enough without forever imagining smoking guns morphing into mushroom clouds. There you

have it: my seven "caps" to contain our gushing support for permanent war. No one said it would be easy. Just ask BP how easy it is to cap one out-of-control gusher.

Nonetheless, if we as a society aren't willing to work hard for actual change—indeed, to demand it—we'll be on that military escalatory curve until we implode. And that way madness lies.

War Is Sometimes Necessary to Ensure Peace

Barack Obama

Barack Obama is the forty-fourth president of the United States.

In the following remarks, delivered upon his receipt of the Nobel Peace Prize, Obama argues that war is sometimes necessary to establish and preserve peace. He says that war has been around for all of recorded history but asserts that international institutions and international norms can help to contain war, to delimit when it is acceptable, and to ensure that it be fought as humanely as possible. Obama says that as president of the United States he has a responsibility to defend his country. He argues that evil exists and that nations need to be ready to resist it. He suggests that such resistance is a better preserver of peace than a determination to never fight in any instance.

Perhaps the most profound issue surrounding my receipt of [the Nobel Peace Prize] is the fact that I am the Commander-in-Chief of the military of a nation in the midst of two wars. One of these wars [in Iraq] is winding down. The other [in Afghanistan] is a conflict that America did not seek; one in which we are joined by 42 other countries—including Norway [sponsor and site of the Peace Prize bestowal]—in an effort to defend ourselves and all nations from further attacks.

War in the Past

Still, we are at war, and I'm responsible for the deployment of thousands of young Americans to battle in a distant land. Some will kill, and some will be killed. And so I come here

Barack Obama, "Remarks by the President at the Acceptance of the Nobel Peace Prize," Whitehouse.gov, December 10, 2009. http://www.whitehouse.gov/the-press-office/remarks-president-acceptance-nobel-peace-prize.

with an acute sense of the costs of armed conflict—filled with difficult questions about the relationship between war and peace, and our effort to replace one with the other.

Now these questions are not new. War, in one form or another, appeared with the first man. At the dawn of history, its morality was not questioned; it was simply a fact, like drought or disease—the manner in which tribes and then civilizations sought power and settled their differences.

And over time, as codes of law sought to control violence within groups, so did philosophers and clerics and statesmen seek to regulate the destructive power of war. The concept of a "just war" emerged, suggesting that war is justified only when certain conditions were met: if it is waged as a last resort or in self-defense; if the force used is proportional; and if, whenever possible, civilians are spared from violence.

Of course, we know that for most of history, this concept of "just war" was rarely observed. The capacity of human beings to think up new ways to kill one another proved inexhaustible, as did our capacity to exempt from mercy those who look different or pray to a different God. Wars between armies gave way to wars between nations—total wars in which the distinction between combatant and civilian became blurred. In the span of 30 years, such carnage would twice engulf this continent. And while it's hard to conceive of a cause more just than the defeat of the Third Reich and the Axis powers, World War II was a conflict in which the total number of civilians who died exceeded the number of soldiers who perished.

In the wake of such destruction, and with the advent of the nuclear age, it became clear to victor and vanquished alike that the world needed institutions to prevent another world war. And so, a quarter century after the United States Senate rejected the League of Nations—an idea for which [President] Woodrow Wilson received this prize—America led the world in constructing an architecture to keep the peace: a Marshall

Plan [for rebuilding European economies after WWII] and a United Nations [U.N.], mechanisms to govern the waging of war, treaties to protect human rights, prevent genocide, restrict the most dangerous weapons.

In many ways, these efforts succeeded. Yes, terrible wars have been fought, and atrocities committed. But there has been no Third World War. The Cold War ended with jubilant crowds dismantling a wall. Commerce has stitched much of the world together. Billions have been lifted from poverty. The ideals of liberty and self-determination, equality and the rule of law have haltingly advanced. We are the heirs of the fortitude and foresight of generations past, and it is a legacy for which my own country is rightfully proud.

New Threats

And yet, a decade into a new century, this old architecture is buckling under the weight of new threats. The world may no longer shudder at the prospect of war between two nuclear superpowers, but proliferation may increase the risk of catastrophe. Terrorism has long been a tactic, but modern technology allows a few small men with outsized rage to murder innocents on a horrific scale.

Moreover, wars between nations have increasingly given way to wars within nations. The resurgence of ethnic or sectarian conflicts; the growth of secessionist movements, insurgencies, and failed states—all these things have increasingly trapped civilians in unending chaos. In today's wars, many more civilians are killed than soldiers; the seeds of future conflict are sown, economies are wrecked, civil societies torn asunder, refugees amassed, children scarred.

I do not bring with me today a definitive solution to the problems of war. What I do know is that meeting these challenges will require the same vision, hard work, and persistence of those men and women who acted so boldly decades ago.

And it will require us to think in new ways about the notions of just war and the imperatives of a just peace.

We must begin by acknowledging the hard truth: We will not eradicate violent conflict in our lifetimes. There will be times when nations—acting individually or in concert—will find the use of force not only necessary but morally justified.

I make this statement mindful of what [civil rights activist] Martin Luther King Jr. said in this same ceremony years ago: "Violence never brings permanent peace. It solves no social problem: it merely creates new and more complicated ones." As someone who stands here as a direct consequence of Dr. King's life work, I am living testimony to the moral force of non-violence. I know there's nothing weak—nothing passive—nothing naïve—in the creed and lives of [Indian non-violent activist Mohandas] Gandhi and King.

But as a head of state sworn to protect and defend my nation, I cannot be guided by their examples alone. I face the world as it is, and cannot stand idle in the face of threats to the American people. For make no mistake: Evil does exist in the world. A non-violent movement could not have halted [German leader Adolf] Hitler's armies. Negotiations cannot convince [terrorist group] al Qaeda's leaders to lay down their arms. To say that force may sometimes be necessary is not a call to cynicism—it is a recognition of history; the imperfections of man and the limits of reason.

I raise this point, I begin with this point because in many countries there is a deep ambivalence about military action today, no matter what the cause. And at times, this is joined by a reflexive suspicion of America, the world's sole military superpower.

Security Through Strength

But the world must remember that it was not simply international institutions—not just treaties and declarations—that brought stability to a post-World War II world. Whatever mis-

After receiving the Nobel Peace Prize, President Barack Obama spoke at the 2009 ceremony in Oslo, Norway. © Scott London/Alamy.

takes we have made, the plain fact is this: The United States of America has helped underwrite global security for more than six decades with the blood of our citizens and the strength of our arms. The service and sacrifice of our men and women in uniform has promoted peace and prosperity from Germany to Korea, and enabled democracy to take hold in places like the Balkans. We have borne this burden not because we seek to impose our will. We have done so out of enlightened self-interest—because we seek a better future for our children and grandchildren, and we believe that their lives will be better if others' children and grandchildren can live in freedom and prosperity.

So yes, the instruments of war do have a role to play in preserving the peace. And yet this truth must coexist with another—that no matter how justified, war promises human tragedy. The soldier's courage and sacrifice is full of glory, expressing devotion to country, to cause, to comrades in arms. But war itself is never glorious, and we must never trumpet it as such.

So part of our challenge is reconciling these two seemingly inreconcilable truths—that war is sometimes necessary, and war at some level is an expression of human folly. Concretely, we must direct our effort to the task that President [John F.] Kennedy called for long ago. "Let us focus," he said, "on a more practical, more attainable peace, based not on a sudden revolution in human nature but on a gradual evolution in human institutions." A gradual evolution of human institutions.

What might this evolution look like? What might these practical steps be?

To begin with, I believe that all nations—strong and weak alike—must adhere to standards that govern the use of force. I—like any head of state—reserve the right to act unilaterally if necessary to defend my nation. Nevertheless, I am convinced that adhering to standards, international standards, strengthens those who do, and isolates and weakens those who don't.

The world rallied around America after the 9/11 attacks [on the World Trade Center and Pentagon in 2001], and continues to support our efforts in Afghanistan, because of the horror of those senseless attacks and the recognized principle of self-defense. Likewise, the world recognized the need to confront [Iraqi dictator] Saddam Hussein when he invaded Kuwait—a consensus that sent a clear message to all about the cost of aggression.

Furthermore, America—in fact, no nation—can insist that others follow the rules of the road if we refuse to follow them ourselves. For when we don't, our actions appear arbitrary and undercut the legitimacy of future interventions, no matter how justified.

And this becomes particularly important when the purpose of military action extends beyond self-defense or the defense of one nation against an aggressor. More and more, we all confront difficult questions about how to prevent the slaughter of civilians by their own government, or to stop a civil war whose violence and suffering can engulf an entire region.

I believe that force can be justified on humanitarian grounds, as it was in the Balkans [in the 1990s], or in other places that have been scarred by war. Inaction tears at our conscience and can lead to more costly intervention later. That's why all responsible nations must embrace the role that militaries with a clear mandate can play to keep the peace.

Peace Requires Responsibility

America's commitment to global security will never waver. But in a world in which threats are more diffuse, and missions more complex, America cannot act alone. America alone cannot secure the peace. This is true in Afghanistan. This is true in failed states like Somalia, where terrorism and piracy is joined by famine and human suffering. And sadly, it will continue to be true in unstable regions for years to come.

The leaders and soldiers of NATO [North Atlantic Treaty Organization] countries, and other friends and allies, demonstrate this truth through the capacity and courage they've shown in Afghanistan. But in many countries, there is a disconnect between the efforts of those who serve and the ambivalence of the broader public. I understand why war is not popular, but I also know this: The belief that peace is desirable is rarely enough to achieve it. Peace requires responsibility. Peace entails sacrifice. That's why NATO continues to be indispensable. That's why we must strengthen U.N. and regional peacekeeping, and not leave the task to a few countries. That's why we honor those who return home from peacekeeping and training abroad to Oslo and Rome; to Ottawa and Sydney; to Dhaka and Kigali—we honor them not as makers of war, but as wagers of peace.

Let me make one final point about the use of force. Even as we make difficult decisions about going to war, we must also think clearly about how we fight it. The Nobel Committee recognized this truth in awarding its first prize for peace to Henry Dunant—the founder of the Red Cross, and a driving force behind the Geneva Conventions.

Where force is necessary, we have a moral and strategic interest in binding ourselves to certain rules of conduct. And even as we confront a vicious adversary that abides by no rules, I believe the United States of America must remain a standard bearer in the conduct of war. That is what makes us different from those whom we fight. That is a source of our strength. That is why I prohibited torture. That is why I ordered the prison at Guantanamo Bay [housing terrorist suspects] closed. And that is why I have reaffirmed America's commitment to abide by the Geneva Conventions. We lose ourselves when we compromise the very ideals that we fight to defend. (Applause.) And we honor—we honor those ideals by upholding them not when it's easy, but when it is hard.

Pacifism Remains a Worthy Alternative

Colman McCarthy

Colman McCarthy is an American journalist, teacher, lecturer, pacifist, and long-time peace activist, who directs the Center for Teaching Peace in Washington, DC.

In the following essay, Colman McCarthy discusses the responses of national political and military leaders and of pacifists to the September 11 attacks of 2001. McCarthy describes the response of national political leaders as advocating warism and violence. In so doing the US leaders and military glamorize the military action with noble names, demonize the enemy with bad names, victimize helpless citizens in the target countries with their weapons, and rationalize the action as the result of provocation. McCarthy proposes instead to use peaceful political, legal, and moral solutions. The political solution involves negotiation, compromise, and reconciliation to stop the killing. The legal solution would involve due process in American and world courts against leaders who incite violence. The moral solution involves forgiving the attackers and asking them to forgive the wrongs that prompted their use of violence. Although pacifists and pacifist organizations have pursued these political, legal, and moral solutions for a long time, their ideals are ignored by the popular media. Nevertheless, McCarthy plans to continue pursuing these solutions.

Since the attacks of Sept. 11, and Oct. 7 when retaliating U.S. pilots began bombing people and buildings in Afghanistan, those of us who are pacifists have found ourselves

Colman McCarthy, "Pacifism Remains a Worthy Alternative," *National Catholic Reporter* , vol. 38, no. 4, November 16, 2001, p. 19. All rights reserved. Reprinted by permission of National Catholic Reporter, 115 E. Armour Blvd., Kansas City, MO 64111. www.ncronline.org.

denounced for bystanding in a time of national peril. We are scorned for not waving flags or supporting the president and his war council. We are damned for being complicit in evil, which is what pacifism, to many critics, clearly is.

The script is followed, as written by Hermann Goering, the Nazi leader: "The people can always be brought to do the bidding of the leaders. That is easy. All you do is tell them they are being attacked and denounce the pacifists for lack of patriotism."

For 20 years, I've taught pacifism and nonviolence—its history, methods and practitioners—to more than 5,000 high school, university, law school and prison students. During those two decades, U.S. presidents, members of Congress and military leaders have also been teaching: warism and violence. Their classroom has been the national lectern of Washington from which a lesson plan has sent American troops to kill people or threaten to kill people in nearly a dozen foreign sites: Lebanon in 1982, Grenada in 1983, Libya in 1986, Panama in 1989, the Persian Gulf in 1990 to present. Somalia in 1992, Haiti in 1994, Sudan in 1998, Afghanistan in 1998, Yugoslavia in 1999, and Afghanistan in 2001.

A familiar pattern has been followed: glamorize, demonize, victimize, rationalize.

U.S. leaders glamorize their interventions by naming them Operation Just Cause (Panama), Operation Restore Hope (Somalia), Operation Desert Storm (Persian Gulf). They demonize the latest enemy: Panama's Noriega was "a drug kingpin," Somalia's General Aidid "a warlord," Saddam Hussein "another Hitler," bin Laden "the evildoer." U.S. pilots victimize defenseless citizens who are trapped in those countries and helpless to escape the bombing runs. Finally, it is all rationalized: Americans are a peace-loving people but, if pushed, will take action.

During World War II, some pacifists tried to become conscientious objectors. In this photograph from 1940, Francis Hall, far right, a religious pacifist, is taking part in a test tribunal for conscientious objectors in New York. Second from the left is Evan W. Thomas, the chairman of the New York War Resisters League, a pacifist organization mentioned in the viewpoint. © AP Images/Anthony Camerano.

In the current war, pacifists are asked, often goadingly, "Ok, you're opposed to violence, but what's your solution instead?"

Fair question. We have a three-part answer based on political, legal and moral solutions.

The political response to Sept. 11 would have been to follow the U.S. government's longtime advice to Israeli and Palestinian leaders: talk to each other, negotiate, deal, compromise, stop the killing and reconcile. The same advice has been repeatedly dispensed to the factions in Northern Ireland. If that advice is fit for those conflicts, why not for ours with the Taliban government, which the U.S. armed and supported in the 1980s during the Afghanistan-Soviet war. Other precedents exist for nonviolent political responses. In the early

1970s, Richard Nixon dealt, negotiated and compromised with the once-demonized Chinese government. In the mid-1980s, Ronald Reagan did the same with the evil empire Russians. Both communist regimes were once portrayed as out to annihilate the U.S., threats far more lethal than the current demons, the ranting ragtag Talibans. Now Russia and China are trading partners.

The legal response to Sept. 11 is to use international law and the world court at the Hague, where due process now has Slobodan Milosevic on trial. Due process brought Manuel Noriega to a federal court in Florida and imprisonment. It recently led to life sentences from a New York court for those responsible for the first attack on the World Trade Center.

The moral response would be to follow the core teachings of the historical figure who President Bush claimed during his candidacy he most looked to for guidance, Jesus: forgive the Sept. 11 attackers for their violence, ask them to forgive the U.S. government for its long history of military and economic violence, and then seek reconciliation through mutual dialogue, not one-sided monologue.

Political, legal and moral responses have been proposed by a long list of pacifists and pacifist organizations for centuries: Mahatma Gandhi, Martin Luther King Jr., Leo Tolstoy, Dorothy Day, Helen Balch, Jeannette Rankin, A. J. Muste, Abdul Aziz Said, Mubarak Awad, Isaiah, Eugene Debs, David Dellinger, Gene Sharp, Philip and Fr. Daniel Berrigan, Andre Trocme, David McReynolds, Michael Nagler, Michael True, John Dear, Thomas Merton, Thich Nhat Hanh, Joan Baez, Adolfo Perez Esquivel, Vincent Harding, Maired Corrigan, Mulford Sibley, Joan Bondurant, the Fellowship of Reconciliation, the Catholic Worker, the War Resisters League, Pax Christi, Quakers, Mennonites, the Church of the Brethren, the Bruderhofs, and many others.

The ideas and ideals of these pacifists are either unknown or casually dismissed by much of the public. Only a few schools pay academic heed to alternatives to violence. The rest are content to graduate peace illiterates year after year. Rarely are pacifists given space on the nation's op-ed pages, or air-time on radio and television programs. During the Persian Gulf War, a survey found that the four television networks ran 738 interviews with experts analyzing the conduct of the war. Only one interviewee was from a major peace group opposing the war. For the media, that was balance: 737 to one.

It appears to be no different today, with each network having its pet retired general on hand for a nightly strategy rap on how to flush out the slippery bin Laden and his fellow cave dwellers.

My own plan is to keep teaching and writing, and resisting the urge to blame those who believe that violence is the solution to conflict, whether among nations or in families and neighborhoods. I blame only one person for the persistence of violence: myself. If I work to be a better husband, father, teacher, writer and informed citizen, I've done all I can to try to decrease the world's violence and increase its peace.

Admittedly, it's not much. But while few of us are called on to do great things, all of us can do small things in a great way.

For Further Discussion

1. In Chapter 1, Rob Ruggenberg discusses Hitler's and Erich Maria Remarque's experiences during World War I. How long was Remarque in combat? Does it seem as if he would know enough to discuss the war as he does in *All Quiet on the Western Front*? Is there a minimum amount of war experience a person needs to have before he or she talks about war? When talking about the meaning of war, should we give more weight to the words of those who have fought, such as Remarque or Hitler? Explain your answer.

2. In his book *The Great War and Modern Memory*, Paul Fussell says that Remarque does not present the reality of war, but instead uses "the whole frenzied machinery of Gothic romance." In particular, Fussell points to Chapter 4 in the novel, where the hero is shelled in a cemetery, and Paul and his friends save themselves by crawling into coffins. Do you agree that Remarque is using overblown horror effects to describe the war? Or does his depiction seem realistic? Use details from the book to support your argument as well as quotes from the arguments of Tobey C. Herzog and J.C. Squire in Chapter 2.

3. Do you think *All Quiet* is a pacifist book or not? Use details from the Remarque's book to defend your argument. See also the arguments of Brian Murdoch, Elisabeth Krimmer, Gregor Dallas, and Stuart A. Scheingold in Chapter 2.

4. Do you believe war is sometimes needed to preserve peace, or can only peace lead to peace? Draw on specific details and reasoning from viewpoints by Steven Pinker, William J. Astore, Barack Obama, and Colman McCarthy in Chapter 3 to make your case.

For Further Reading

Pat Barker, *Regeneration*, 1991.

Stephen Crane, *The Red Badge of Courage*, 1895.

Robert Graves, *Goodbye to All That*, 1929.

Joseph Heller, *Catch-22*, 1961.

Ernest Hemingway, *A Farewell to Arms*, 1929.

Ernst Junger, *The Storm of Steel*, 1920.

Joy Kogawa, *Obasan*, 1981.

Erich Maria Remarque, *The Road Back*, 1931.

Erich Maria Remarque, *Three Comrades*, 1937.

Kurt Vonnegut, *Slaughterhouse-Five*, 1969.

Rebecca West, *The Return of the Soldier*, 1918.

Bibliography

Books

Peter Englund   *The Beauty and the Sorrow: An Intimate History of the First World War.* Trans. Peter Graves. New York: Knopf, 2011.

Niall Ferguson   *The Pity of War: Explaining World War I.* New York: Penguin, 1999.

Richard Arthur Firda   *"All Quiet on the Western Front": Literary Analysis and Cultural Context.* Boston: Twayne, 1993.

Paul Fussell   *The Great War and Modern Memory.* New York: Oxford University Press, 1975.

Julie Gilbert   *Opposite Attraction: The Lives of Erich Maria Remarque and Paulette Goddard.* New York: Pantheon, 1995.

Adam Hochschild   *To End All Wars: A Story of Loyalty and Rebellion, 1914–1918.* New York: Houghton Mifflin Harcourt, 2011.

John Keegan   *The Face of Battle: A Study of Agincourt, Waterloo, and the Somme.* London: Faber and Faber, 1976.

Mark Kurlansky   *Nonviolence: The History of a Dangerous Idea.* New York: Modern Library, 2006.

Eric J. Leed   *No Man's Land: Combat & Identity in World War I.* Cambridge: Cambridge University Press, 1979.

Hans Wagener   *Understanding Erich Maria Remarque.* Columbia: University of South Carolina Press, 1991.

Periodicals and Internet Sources

Caroline   "The Shock of War," *Smithsonian*
Alexander   *Magazine*, September 2010.
                      www.smithsonianmag.com/history
                      -archaeology/The-Shock-of-War.html.

Joanna Bourke   "Shell Shock During World War One," *BBC*, March 10, 2011. www.bbc.co.uk/history/worldwars /wwone/shellshock_01.shtml.

Andrew Brown   "Steven Pinker's Book Is a Comfort Blanket for the Smug," *Guardian* (Manchester, UK), November 8, 2011. www.guardian.co.uk /commentisfree/2011/nov/08/steven -pinker-better-angels-of-our-nature.

Helen Cleary   "The Human Face of War: The German Officer," *BBC*, March 10, 2011. www.bbc.co.uk/history /worldwars/wwone/humanfaceofwar _gallery_04.shtml.

| Maureen Corrigan | "WWI: A Moral Contest Between Pacifists and Soldiers," National Public Radio, May 4, 2011. www.npr.org/2011/05/04 /135983570/wwi-a-moral-contest -between-pacifists-and-soldiers. |

| Modris Eksteins | *"All Quiet on the Western Front* and the Fate of a War," *Journal of Contemporary History,* April 1980. |

| Modris Eksteins | "War, Memory, and Politics: The Fate of the Film *All Quiet on the Western Front,"* *Central European History,* vol. 13, 1980. |

| Glenn Greenwald | "The Strange Consensus on Obama's Nobel Address," *Salon,* December 11, 2009. www.salon.com /2009/12/11/obama_127/singleton/. |

| Robin Marantz Henig | "Is Violence Finished?," Daily Beast, October 3, 2011. www.thedailybeast.com /newsweek/2011/10/02/steven -pinker-s-better-angels-of-our -nature-review.html. |

| John B. Judis | "Obama, Niebuhr, and U.S. Politics," *New Republic,* December 13, 2009. www.tnr.com/blog/the-plank/obama -niebuhr-and-us-politics. |

| Ramzi Kysia | "A Pacifist Critique of Obama's Nobel Lecture," *Counterpunch,* December 11–13, 2009. www.counterpunch.org/2009/12/11 /a-pacifist-critique-of-obama-s-nobel -lecture/. |

Eric J. Leed   "Class and Disillusionment in World
                      War I," *Journal of Modern History*,
                      December 1978.

New York Times   "Erich Maria Remarque Is Dead;
                      Novels Recorded Agony of War,"
                      September 26, 1970.
                      www.nytimes.com/learning/general
                      /onthisday/bday/0622.html.

New York   "The Life and Writings of Erich
University   Maria Remarque," n.d.
                      www.nyu.edu/library/bobst/research
                      /fales/exhibits/remarque/documents
                      /intro.html.

Louisa Thomas   "Give Pacifism a Chance," *New York
                      Times*, August 27, 2011.
                      www.nytimes.com/2011/08/28
                      /opinion/sunday/what-is-pacifism
                      -good-for.html?pagewanted=all.

Index

CPSIA information can be obtained
at www.ICGtesting.com
Printed in the USA
FFOW05n2255220813
1631FF

9 780737 763928